Award-winning writer, television broadcaster and author of numerous bestsellers, **Leslie Kenton** is described in the press as 'the guru of health and fitness' and 'the most original voice in health'. A shining example of energy and commitment, she is highly respected for her thorough reporting. Leslie was born in California. She is the daughter of jazz musician Stan Kenton and Violet Peters, a painter. After leaving Stanford University she journeyed to Europe in her early twenties, settling first in Paris then in Britain where she has since remained. She has raised four children on her own by working as a television broadcaster, novelist, writer and teacher on health and for fourteen years she was an editor at *Harpers & Queen*.

Leslie's writing on mainstream health is internationally known and has appeared in *Vogue*, the *Sunday Times*, *Cosmopolitan* and the *Daily Mail*. She is the author of many other health books including: *The Joy of Beauty*, *Ultrahealth*, *Raw Energy* and *Raw Energy Recipes* – co-authored with her daughter Susannah – *Ageless Ageing*, *The Biogenic Diet*, *Cellulite Revolution*, *10 Day Clean-up Plan*, *Endless Energy*, *Nature's Child* and the *10 Day De-stress Plan*. She turned to fiction with *Ludwig* – her first novel. Former consultant to a medical corporation in the USA and to the Open University's Centre of Continuing Education, Leslie has won several awards for her writing including the PPA 'Technical Writer of the Year'. Her work was honoured by her being asked to deliver the McCarrison Lecture at the Royal Society of Medicine. In recent years she has become increasingly concerned not only with the process of enhancing individual health but also with re-establishing bonds with the earth as a part of helping to heal the planet. Leslie now lives in West Wales in an eighteenth-century house overlooking the sea, once inhabited by Virginia Woolf.

Lean
Revolution

Eat more to shed fat
the energy way

Leslie Kenton

EBURY PRESS • LONDON

3 5 7 9 10 8 6 4 2

First published in the United Kingdom in 1994 by
Ebury Press
Random House
20 Vauxhall Bridge Road
London SW1V 2SA

Random House Australia (Pty) Limited
20 Alfred Street, Milsons Point, Sydney,
New South Wales 2061, Australia

Random House New Zealand Limited
18 Poland Road, Glenfield,
Auckland 10, New Zealand

Random House South Africa (Pty) Limited
PO Box 337, Bergvlei, South Africa

Random House Canada
1265 Aerowood Drive, Mississauga,
Ontario L4W IB9, Canada

Random House UK Limited Reg. No 954009

A CIP catalogue record for this book is available
from the British Library.

0 09 178415 8

Typeset from author's disks by Clive Dorman & Co.

Printed and bound in Great Britain by Clays Limited, StIves plc.

Papers used by Ebury Press are natural recyclable products made
from wood grown in sustainable forests.

For Clancy

with my love

The material in this book is intended for information purposes only. None of the suggestions or information is meant in any way to be prescriptive. Any attempt to treat a medical condition should always come under the direction of a competent physician – and neither the publisher nor I can accept responsibility for injuries or illness arising out of a failure by a reader to take medical advice. I am only a reporter. I also have a profound interest in helping myself and others to maximize potentials for positive health which includes being able to live at a high level of energy, intelligence and creativity. For all three are expressions of harmony within a living organic system.

Acknowledgements

It would take another book to list all of the generous physicians and scientists who have taught me what lies within. I want however to say a special thanks to a few without whom my search for answers would never have born fruits: Dr Gordon Latto, Dr Barbara Latto, Dr Philip Kilsby, Dr Andrew Strigner, Dr Peter Mansfield, Dr Dagmar Liechti von Brasch, Sang Lee MD, Milton Crane MD, Dr Vince Quas, Dr Michael Colgan, Vincent Gardner MD, Warren Peters MD, Dr Stoy Procter, and Vernon Foster MD. I also want to thank Henry Martin for his enormous generosity of spirit and help in chasing down answers to my lengthy lists of questions, Carole Marno for her inspiration and wisdom, Joanna Sheehan for caring so much about producing something good and – most of all – my assistant Yvette Brown, better known as The Fox, for her intelligence, her sense of humour and her willingness to work seven days a week, sixteen hours a day if necessary just to help me get the job done

Leslie Kenton
Pembrokeshire 1994

Contents

MEASUREMENTS & QUANTITIES

I have given approximate measurements in the recipes as cupfuls (an ordinary cup holds about 225 ml or 8 fluid ounces), tablespoons, teaspoons, pinches and so on. Each time you make a recipe it will be slightly different, which is the whole fun of cooking and eating. Where measuring is important, I have given the imperial measurement as well as the metric. Most of the recipes are designed to feed 4 people. As the quantities are approximate, the amounts can easily be adjusted to suit your own particular needs.

In the main text I have mainly used metric measurements except where the original research was done in pounds and ounces, or the statistics were quoted in gallons or feet and inches. It would be artificial in those cases to convert to metric for the sake of it. Here are a few metric/imperial equivalents which you may find useful.

Weight

28 grams	= 1 ounce
112 grams	= ¼ lb
450 grams	= 1 lb
1 kilogram	= 2.2 lb

Volume

570 ml	= 1 pint
1 litre	= 1¾ pints
4.5 litres	= 1 gallon

Length

2.5 cm	= 1 inch
30 cm	= 1 foot
1 metre/100cm	= 39 inches/3.3 feet
1.6 kilometres	= 1 mile

Chapter One

Strike For Freedom

Within each one of us, thin or fat, there lives a joyous creative spirit. It is the spirit of the child – of life itself – a completely individual nature which is constantly seeking freedom simply to be what it is and to do what it wants to do. The world we live in as we grow up seldom leaves space for that unique spirit to fully develop. Our parents, our education, our culture is continually feeding us with rules about what we should and shouldn't do – should and shouldn't be. It is a little like getting up each morning and having to put on your strait jacket before you begin the day. For many people – especially women – weight control has become part of that strait jacket. They worry constantly about how or what to eat or not to eat. They agonize over tiny amounts of weight gained or lost and treat themselves like naughty children who need controlling lest they get out of hand and eat something they shouldn't.

A person in any kind of strait jacket is a person disempowered. It is a person who does not trust himself or herself and who to a greater or lesser degree lives in fear – fear of food, fear of what he or she might do, fear of disapproval from a society impassioned by notions of thinness. I have known that struggle. I have lived it myself and I see evidence of it all around me in women caught in the jaws of bulimia, anorexia or compulsive eating, and in men who over-indulge in alcohol or fatty foods, and who are struck down by a heart attack in the prime of life. This has always seemed a terrible waste.

Power for Change

Twenty years ago I began to ask questions like: why do so many people struggle with weight in our society when the vast majority in other cultures never even seem to grow fat? What causes the distortions to our bodies not only in body size and fat deposits, but also in our biochemistry? Is it really weakness of character or lack of will power that makes us all eat too much and gain weight? And – most important of all – is there a way of eating and living that enables someone who is carrying around too much fat to eat and live so that whatever distortions have already appeared will disappear quite naturally as part of the process of regenerating the body through food and exercise?

I went looking for answers. I set out to discover what has brought about the widespread obesity and weight problems that we experience in the Western world. I looked at the work of Sir Robert McCarrison who initiated the first investigations into the relationship between diet and the development of disease, including obesity. I investigated the theories and practices of Max Bircher-Benner MD who created the Bircher-Benner clinic in Zürich which is now run by the Swiss government, where for almost a century people suffering from weight and other degenerative conditions have gone to find them-selves transformed by changing the way that they live and eat. In the Seventies I became fascinated by the work in lifestyle change as a means of reversing degenerative diseases that was being carried out at the Longevity Center of Nathan Pritiken in California, where 85 per cent of the patients with hypertension were able within four weeks to restore their blood pressure to normal and get off medication as a result of changes in diet and lifestyle alone. I discovered that at another centre in California – Loma Linda University – research and health education programmes were being carried out with similar results. There, overweight people shed their excess fat without counting calories but by shifting the kinds of foods they eat away from high-fat, high-protein convenience foods to a low-fat diet based on whole grains, legumes, vegetables and fruit. I was surprised to learn, too, that, once the oppressive influence of the Western diet is eliminated, even many diabetics who have been on 50, 60, 70 or 80 units of insulin for 5 to 10 years are able to restore their insulin production to normal within weeks.

Super Healthy

During the course of my investigations I became fascinated by one particular group of people – the Seventh Day Adventists – a religious group in the West replete with doctors and scientists who, since the nineteenth century, have been exploring in depth the relationship between such things as diet, exercise, trust and health. Adventists' teaching is based on the notion that to evolve spiritually one needs to ensure that the body is strong, clean and healthy and that the brain – as part of the body – functions properly. Few Adventists smoke. They eat a lot less animal fat and sugar than does the general population. Their age-adjusted death rates for heart disease and cancer are way below the national average in the United States. Some are total vegetarians, other consume animal products. I was also intrigued to find out that the death rate for those that are complete vegetarians is significantly lower again than those who incorporate meat into what is otherwise a very good diet. Another interesting finding from a large-scale study of Adventist health is that although the lacto-ovo vegetarians – that is those who eat eggs and milk – have a death rate for cancer and heart disease lower than the meat eaters, those who

11

are complete vegans – that is those who eat no milk products or eggs – have the lowest of all. Their rate of colon cancer is so low, in fact, that it is only about 50 per cent of the general US population. When vegan Adventists do develop heart disease it tends to occur ten years later than in the rest of the Western world. Numerous studies of other groups of people all over the world have shown that when men and women living on a low-fat diet, such as the Japanese, migrate to Western countries and alter their diet they very quickly develop our degenerative diseases, including obesity. Rates of colon cancer also soar as does breast cancer. In short, when people eat differently they produce different disease patterns. Being overweight, just like our other degenerative conditions, I realized, is really a problem of lifestyle.

Proof of the Pudding

So I read many books and papers, listened to dozens of lectures from physicians and scientists – many of them Adventists – and interviewed a number of doctors personally who are involved in the new exciting field of *lifestyle medicine*. I was impressed by their work and by the work of many others including, in particular, Dean Ornish MD, director of the Preventative Medicine Research Institute in Sausalito, California. Ornish and his colleagues measured the effect of comprehensive lifestyle changes on patients with coronary artery disease by introducing them to a meat, fish and poultry-free ultra-low-fat vegetarian diet of fruits, vegetables, grains, legumes and soya bean products coupled with stress management sessions and regular exercise. After a year over 80 per cent of the patients had experienced regression of their arterial fatty deposits without the use of drugs while the control patients, with no lifestyle intervention, experienced nothing but a substantial progression of their illness. Ornish's work has recently been widely publicized. It is highly praised and is much respected. As a result, his programme has just become the first non-surgical, non-pharmaceutical therapy for heart disease to qualify for American insurance reimbursement – something that has never happened before in the history of Western medicine. The message from all of this rang loud and clear. For the evidence grows daily that our high-sugar, high-fat, high-protein diet of processed foods is responsible for massive amounts of destruction to the human body and, interestingly enough, the diets used for both prevention and reversal of various kinds of degeneration do not vary greatly from disease to disease. It is a way of eating which our body quite naturally appears to thrive on – high in grains and fruits, legumes and vegetables, moderate instead of high in protein, and low in fat and processed foods. Eating this way enables the body to function at the highest level of health and wellbeing. Change a person's lifestyle and you can not only largely prevent degenerative conditions of which being overweight is a major one, you can often *reverse* degeneration *after* it has occurred.

What follows in *Lean Revolution* is only a tip of the remarkable iceberg now surfacing as lifestyle medicine. It comes not out of what is called alternative or complementary medicine but from mainstream work done by leading-edge medical doctors in Europe and America. There was a time when physicians like these men and women concerned themselves primarily with the treatment of illness through drugs. Now, far-sighted doctors have turned their attention towards charting exactly how changes in lifestyle can be used to restore high-level health once it has been lost.

Thin for What?

In the Western world we have developed an obsession about changing the shape of our bodies, especially trying to make them thinner. Yet making a body thinner is not always the best thing to do – either for its health or its

13

good looks. A thin body is a wimpish body. It is a body depleted of energy and of power. When you are lean you are strong, you have sleek muscles, good tone, and you can feast heartily on wholesome, natural foods and stay that way. You are also highly resistant to illness and early ageing and you feel comfortable and at ease in your body. It is a very different experience from the anxiety over thinness which disempowers so many men and women. Leanness brings a sense of power with it – a sense of being in control of your own life that is a far cry from the inadequacy many women feel as they continue to battle against weight gain with conventional slimming diets. I believe it is time we forgot about thin and chose instead to *go lean*. This calls for revolution.

To revolutionize means to change completely and fundamentally – your body and your life. It is not a word chosen lightly but because it most accurately describes the powerful positive transformation that takes place in how you look and feel when you throw out convenience foods which are loaded with hidden sugar or junk fats and begin to feed heartily on wholesome low-fat complex carbohydrate foods, drink large quantities of pure water and increase your muscle mass through slow, steady exercise. The word *lean* means 'muscular... containing little or no fat.' Being lean is as different from being thin as the *Lean Revolution* is from all the quick-fix slimming diets you may have tried over the years which have slowly but inexorably eroded your energy and increased the sense of disenchantment with your body.

Go Lean

Cut your calorie intake below the number that your body is burning as energy and you will lose weight. When you have lost enough weight, you will be thin. That is the goal of slimming diets. To be thin means to have a *low body weight*. But in time a thin body becomes a soft body – a body without tone. It is a body prone to fatigue, early ageing and degeneration. It is also a disempowered body – one that needs to be watched carefully lest it eats something forbidden and changes shape again. To be lean means to have a low percentage of *body fat*. A lean body is always smaller in size than a thin body of the same weight since muscle tissue is much denser than fat tissue. Go lean and you gain enormously in energy, stamina and general health. You can also end up looking years younger. And where you once had to watch every calorie you consumed in order not to gain weight, you will be able to eat without worrying about calories.

A rugby player who is 1.8 metres can weigh as much as 100 kilos yet be lean if his muscle-to-fat ratio is very high on the side of muscle. He may have to eat as many as 4,000 calories a day to look and feel his best. His brother, who is the same height, weighs only 75 kilos. He would be considered thin according to the weight tables from insurance companies. Yet he is *not* lean. For he boasts very little muscle and carries a lot of fat. He also leads a sedentary life and eats convenience foods. As a result he has to be very careful about how much he eats. If he takes in more than 1,800 calories a day, the waistline starts to spread dangerously. It works the same with women. A thin woman, 1.6 metres tall, weighs 57 kilos and wears a size 10 dress. But her body is soft since lots of her weight is fat tissue. The same woman, when she becomes lean, will weigh 60 kilos yet only wear a size 8.

Ready... Steady...

Once you commit yourself to a *Lean Revolution* all sorts of good things start to happen. If you have used appetite suppressants you discover that you no longer need them. You begin to shed excess fat and build sleek, firm muscle naturally at a rate that doesn't trigger survival mechanisms which force your body to hold on to its fat stores. You discover you are free to eat with pleasure and enthusiasm as much as your body wants. Soon you find yourself living in a way that supports your health to the highest possible degree and brings you lots of energy, self-confidence and a sense that you are strong enough to meet whatever challenges life has in store for you.

The important question now becomes: are you serious about shedding fat and restoring your body's natural form? This is all the commitment you need to bring about a *Lean Revolution* in your own life. Yet it demands two things: first that you decide to respect yourself and your own life and to live as though you mattered despite whatever feelings of inadequacy, guilt or anything else you happen to be carrying with you. Second, that you begin. The exciting thing about making such a commitment is that the odd binge on chocolate cake becomes an insignificant hiccup along the way. For when you are clear about where you are going, you will discover that the further you travel the more trust you gain in the whole process of lifestyle transformation and the easier it all becomes.

I wanted the complex, scientific information contained in this little book to be accessible. But extensive references to each chapter are available (see p.187) in the hope that doctors and health professionals as well as ordinary people like myself who are keen to understand more deeply the way in which lifestyle affects health and leanness can learn more about the fascinating new field of lifestyle medicine. I hope that what lies within can in some small way help banish the despair of people who, like me, have struggled long with being overweight and believing myself to be powerless. Most of all, I hope that your own *Lean Revolution* will help you realize how much untapped creative power lies within you. One of the remarkable things that takes place as the ratio between lean body tissue and fat shifts in favour of muscle is that men and women alike rediscover a new sense of personal power and freedom. It is my belief that each of us needs to live our power and freedom if we are to find creative answers to the problems facing our rapidly changing society and our increasingly polluted planet.

Chapter Two

Let Diets Die

Being overweight is the *bête noire* of the Western world. It preys on one out of every three people – man, woman and child. Impeccable medical research shows that too much fat on your body can lead to serious degenerative illnesses – heart disease, diabetes, hypertension, arthritis and gout. Overweight people are far more likely than their lean cousins to develop cancer of the colon, cervix, breast, uterus, prostate and ovaries, as well as back trouble. The fatter you grow, the more it depresses your immune system, making you susceptible to infection or invasion and to premature ageing. According to the Framingham Study (one of the largest long-term health studies in the world), even packing three to five extra kilos of fat around your middle results in higher mortality – each extra kilo shaving just over two months off your life. Twenty kilos and you could lose two years.

In the United States 34 million people are now at serious medical risk because they are not just overweight but obese, that is they carry at least 20 per cent too much fat on their bodies. This costs the American people $30.6 billion a year on health care. Once upon a time one could look at US statistics and congratulate ourselves that the rest of the English-speaking world was safe from the excesses of our American cousins. No longer. Thanks to a global proliferation of convenience foods, the spread of fast food restaurants, and a glut of fatty, sugary snacks on the market, Canadians, Britons, Europeans, Australians, New Zealanders and Africans are catching up quick. Throughout the Western world being overweight and its consequent degenerative conditions are now responsible for one in every five deaths.

Slimming Obsession

As our waistlines spread so does anxiety about getting thin. Our growing obsession with quick-fix solutions has actually helped to create the problem. Impeccable medical research has now established that going on and off calorie-restricted weight-loss diets distorts our nutrition and unbalances our metabolism so that we grow fatter and sicker with each passing year. At any moment in time 40–50 per cent of the Western world is dieting. Yet the results of our efforts are not promising: in the past twenty years, on average, each of us has put on five pounds in weight. For women the statistics look even worse. Between the ages of 18 and 40 the average woman sheds five pounds of muscle only to replace it with 23 pounds of fat.

All this is part of the insane world we live in – a world where magazines and newspapers produce endless diet plans, many based on the rampant misinformation which can pervade the multi-billion weight-loss industry. It is an industry which appears more skilful at enhancing its own bank balance than at improving our health and good looks. Magazines which scream at us from one page that we need to be thin to stay young, beautiful and be loved, on the next page entice us to 'sin' with a recipe for Black Forest gâteau. Meanwhile our children spend hours in front of the television being brainwashed by advertisements designed to make them demand more highly processed junk foods – breakfast cereals, sweets, soft drinks and snacks, all of which are chock full of hidden

18

sugars and fats. These nutritionally empty foods carry only one promise: that their generation will be even fatter and less healthy than our own. One thing is for certain: if we are serious about shedding excess body fat permanently and halting the exponential spread of flab in our culture we have been going about it the wrong way.

Forget Calorie Counting

The standard advice about slimming is to count calories. Except that calorie counting doesn't work. Researcher Kelly Brownell in Pennsylvania discovered that animals placed on a low-calorie diet quickly regain weight once the calorie restrictions are removed. It takes them twice as long to lose it the next time around on the same calorie-restricted diet. But it takes less than a third of the time for them to get fat again.

By their very nature, calorie charts themselves are not usually accurate. There can be anywhere between 250 and 500 calories in a piece of chocolate cake depending on its size, the amount of sugar and the quantity of fat used in making it. You can also have no way of knowing how many of the calories in a particular hunk of food will be *bio-available* – that is in a form that your body will absorb. Finally, scientific studies show that the age-old equation which the calorie-counters would have you believe doesn't hold water. It goes something like this: to lose weight all you need to do is cut down on the number of calories by x number each day. When that figure adds up to 3,600 – the calories in one pound of flesh – you will have shed 450 grams or a pound in weight. It may sound good on paper but, for a number of scientifically documented reasons, it is simply not true.

Highly complex physiological mechanisms in your body are involved in fat burning and fat storage. They come into play when you restrict calories. Biochemist and expert in nutrition and exercise, Dr Michael Colgan, President of the Colgan Institute in California, whose total-body approach to weight control is one of the few in the world that actually works (he gets an amazing 80 per cent long-term success rate with his slimmers), once carried out an interesting experiment at the University of Auckland in New Zealand. He took four men and two women keen to lose a few pounds. For six weeks he made them cut the amount of food they ate for lunch exactly in half while carefully monitoring the foods they ate at other times to make sure that they reduced between 250 and 400 calories a day from their normal intake. Then he sat back to watch the pounds fall away. Unfortunately they didn't. At the end of the test period only two subjects had shed any weight at all – three-quarters of a pound in the case of one and 1½ pounds in the other. By the '3,600 rule' these two should have lost at least 2½ pounds and 4½ pounds respectively. While the others taking part, who should have shed between 2¼ and 5½ pounds, had lost nothing at all.

Many slimmers have similar experiences. The sad truth is that slicing calories off your daily menus does not necessarily shave padding from your hips. The human body has far too complex a system of defences designed to protect its fat stores. A similar situation exists for people who are desperate to put *on* weight. They can swallow massive quantities of extra calories to no avail. The inherited capacity of men and women to accumulate fat through over-eating or to shed fat through under-eating varies enormously from person to person. Given the complexity of the physiological dynamics of the human body, this preoccupation with counting calories which has been foisted on us for half a century by books, food manufacturers and slimming clubs is starting to look pretty silly.

Starve to Grow Fat

There is now clear scientific evidence that dieting makes you *gain* weight. This should be written in big red letters over every crash diet – like the government's health warning on cigarettes: dieting trains your body to become fatter. Stick to a calorie-restricted diet for a few weeks and you get thinner. But when you resume your old eating habits, the weight you lost begins to creep back on. Statistics show that between 85 per cent and 90 per cent of all slimmers regain weight lost on low-calorie diets within a year. Sooner or later this regain leads you to try again. Then what is known as the *yo-yo effect* comes about: you lose weight by depriving yourself, regain it when you go back to eat normally again, lose some more, gain it back and so on endlessly. But here's the rub: each time you shed kilos, they are drawn both from your body's fat stores *and* its muscle stores. However, each time you regain it, it comes back as *fat*.

It is an established scientific fact that on a diet of 800-1,200 calories a day up to 45 per cent of the weight you shed does *not* come from your fat stores. It is made up of water and muscle – the result of your body cannibalizing its own lean tissue. That is why (even if you are one of the lucky few who have been able to prevent ballooning up) at the end of a few years of on/off slimming much of your muscle tissue will have been replaced by fat. Your body looks flabby. You may even have gone up a size or two in clothing although you still weigh the same. Body fat is lighter than muscle tissue. When your fat-to-muscle-ratio becomes tipped in favour of fat – as it *inevitably* does in all dedicated slimmers – you can carry more bulk and look bigger even though you weigh less.

Every slimming regime that reduces the body's muscle stock is doomed to failure. For it is only in muscle cells that fat is burnt. Reduce your muscle stock and you decrease the areas in which fat can be burnt. Then you find it harder and harder to lose weight even if, through super-human will, you lower your calorie intake to 1,000 calories or less a day. The more muscle you carry on your body the greater is your capacity for burning calories and the easier it is for you to stay lean. This too should be written in big red letters over every crash diet. The converse is also true: the less muscle tissue in your body the easier it is for you to grow fatter and fatter and the more likely it is that you will stay that way.

Dead Meat

It is not only creeping flab from yo-yo slimming – what obesity expert Jean Meyer calls the 'rhythm method of girth control' – that continues to make you fat either. The inevitable shift in body composition away from muscle tissue towards fat which comes with yo-yo dieting undermines your chances of permanent fat loss in other insidious ways. Your body's fat cells are much less active metabolically than all its other cells. Stores of body fat are a bit like dead meat. They don't burn energy, they just sit there storing it. Muscle cells, on the other hand, are highly active metabolically. It is within the mitochondria of muscles (the body's energy factories, of which there are billions) that energy burning and fat burning take place. When, as a result of yo-yo dieting, you have decreased your muscle tissue and increased your fat stores – even if your weight itself doesn't go up – you also undermine your body's ability to burn fat by decreasing basal metabolic rate (BMR) or the amount of energy your body uses to keep its physiological processes ticking over. A man who weighs 140 kilos but whose body composition is half fat needs the same amount of food to maintain his weight as a man of 80 kilos who is all muscle. To shed fat and re-establish your own natural body form you need to forget calorie counting and concentrate on enhancing muscle.

Meet Your Fat Enzyme

As if all this bad news were not enough, yo-yo dieting makes your body retain fat in yet another way, thanks to an enzyme called *lipoprotein lipase* – your 'fat storage enzyme'. On a low-calorie diet, lipoprotein lipase picks up any excess calories floating in your bloodstream, especially calories from refined sugar, white flour and processed fats and oils, and carries them off to stuff them back into your fat cells in an effort to protect your body from starvation. When you stop dieting the levels of this enzyme remain high for weeks which encourages regain. Then, horrified by the spreading hips or puckering thighs you see when you look in the mirror, you turn to yet another slimming regime in an effort to hold on to your new shape. But your body, sensing that it is losing its energy stores, activates all its ancient biochemical mechanisms – the ones our ancestors used to survive famine. One of the most important is our lipoprotein lipase, whose concentration and action is increased yet again in an effort to hold on to all the fat it can.

Lose-Lose Scenario

This heightened lipoprotein lipase activity as well as the BMR slowdown can go on for months after you have stopped dieting, as your body attempts to get back to what it was before the 'threat'. It latches on to every calorie you consume and tries to store it instead of allowing you to use it as energy. This results in chronic fatigue and can lead you to feel ravenous too. After many years of yo-yo-ing up and down, the triggers for the release of lipoprotein lipase can become so exquisitely sensitive that your body tries to store fat from every calorie you eat. This is a major cause of the fatigue and depression in dieters. They become obsessed with weight-loss yet feel powerless to ever find a way out of the fat-accumulation jungle where restricting calories to 1,200 or even 800 a day doesn't work any more.

Few slimmers are aware that all of this is what has been causing their problems. These are some of the secrets the purveyors of slimming regimes, appetite suppressants and low-calorie foods don't tell you. Most of them don't even *know*. Of course, it must be said that it is not in their best interests to find out. If they did they would have to admit that the 'solutions' they offer us are bogus.

23

Meanwhile slimmers get more depressed, more anxious and more desperate for the next quick-fix solution.

You could, of course, go to a hospital and have your jaw wired so you don't eat. People do. The lengths to which we now go to get rid of our excess weight seem quite incredible. They range from intestinal bypass operations, stomach stapling and liposuction – where fat is sucked from under the skin with the aid of a mini vacuum cleaner – to balloon implantations where a balloon is put into the stomach and then inflated, the idea being that if you feel full you will not be inclined to eat as much. You can lose weight in all these ways. But the same problems apply. Once the wire or balloon is removed you will be back playing the yo-yo game and paying its flabby price in ill health and ravaged looks.

Ruin Your Looks

Some popular diets are nutritionally inadequate to a degree that in the long run they not only contribute to weight *gain* instead of permanent fat loss but can also do serious damage to your body and to your looks. Dr Paul La Chance and Michelle Fisher at the department of Food Science at Rutgers University analysed a large number of the most popular diets – from Scarsdale to F Plan – including many of the more restrictive regimes. They discovered that nutritionally virtually all are seriously deficient in fibre, vitamins and minerals. Let's get specific.

Low-carbohydrate/high protein diets consist of eating meals that are high in protein, meat, eggs, fish, cheese etc. – and moderate-to-high in fat plus a few vegetables, while cutting out starches like bread and pasta and sweets. There is nothing new about feeding people meat, fish and eggs and forbidding them breads, cakes and chocolate creams to get them to shed weight. The high-pro-low-carb diet was first used way back in the nineteenth century by the British surgeon William Harvey. You can lose weight on it – and fast too. But much of the weight you lose will be water. Also your muscle stores are cannibalized and your health can be undermined in the process. These regimes force your body to shed glycogen from your tissues – your energy stores. Glycogen is itself highly hydrated – hence the quick weight loss from water. But you will not lose fat so easily. High-pro-low-carb stimulates your body to produce more anti-diuretic hormone so you will tend to hold on to every drop of water you take in. It also causes toxic waste substances called ketone bodies to accumulate in your system which can lead to a loss of minerals from your bones, nails and hair – weakening and softening them. And it contributes to the development of pre-menstrual syndrome and menopausal problems, gout and kidney failure, including the growth of kidney stones. Finally, high-pro-low-carb diets, by their very nature, contain a lot of fat which accumulates as plaque in your arteries. Steer clear of them.

Lousy Nutrition

A major reason why many slimming regimes are nutritionally inadequate is that they are based not on real food – vegetables, fruits, grains and legumes grown on healthy soils – but rather on manufactured foods and chemical formulas. After a few years of going on and off these regimes your supplies of essential minerals and trace elements becomes unbalanced and depleted. Sooner or later your body begins to rebel. This can come in the form of PMT or fatigue, irritability or susceptibility to illness.

The burning of calories for energy, the production of new hormones for digestion or for making neurotransmitters in the brain which make you think and feel right – none of these can work properly without optimal supplies of minerals and trace elements. As the work of La Chance, Fisher and others clearly shows, most slimming diets don't supply them. And as Dr Michael Colgan points out: 'Combined with the food and calorie restrictions that these diets impose, such deficiencies are an invitation to illness.' Following any regime deficient in vitamins, minerals and trace elements found in adequate quantities of wholesome foods, is a sure way to set yourself up for fatigue, depression, lowered immunity and the relentless development of an unattractive face and body as the years pass.

La Chance and Fisher conclude that other popular quick-loss diets which severely restrict the variety of foods available to you are particularly poor. Going on such regimes often result in dizziness, headaches and potassium deficiency. The most you can achieve is *quick and temporary* weight loss. But you pay the piper. Even more absurd are the 'Water Diets', the 'Grapefruit Diets', and other silly fads which continue to raise their ugly heads in glossy magazines and newspapers. They are incapable of supporting health and good looks even short term. And, as far as the liquid meal replacements and their close-cousins, the very low-calorie diets are concerned, despite what they tell you on the label, they are both nutritionally inadequate and ineffective for lasting weight control. Yet diets abound. Last month I counted 46 new ones in British magazines alone. For dieting is big business.

Pill Popping Won't Do It

Appetite suppressants are no better. Those available on prescription are amphetamines which carry with them a huge list of unhealthy side effects including depression, insomnia, dry mouth, drug dependence and abuse. The best known of the over-the-counter variety are based on phenylpropanolamine (PPA), a stimulant which curbs appetite thanks to its action on the hypothalamus. After taking PPA for a while your body develops a tolerance to it and begins to metabolize and excrete the chemical very quickly. Noticing this, many slimmers figure they need to take ever bigger doses to get any effect. Don't. PPA can dangerously raise blood pressure in some people. It has also caused haemorrhaging and been associated with other serious side effects including strokes.

Even diuretics are touted as an aid to weight loss. These pills make your body shed water so you weigh less when you step on the scales. But water loss has nothing to do with fat loss. In fact you may be surprised to find out that you *need* water – lots of it – to shed fat and keep it off (see Chapter 7). The one thing diuretics *will* make you shed is potassium. And the loss of this important mineral can have serious long-term consequences for your health including fatigue and high blood pressure. Artificial sweeteners don't help either, nor do foods like diet colas containing them. Studies show that calories you save by using them are spent in extra eating. For they do not satisfy the tongue, the mouth or the stomach. Many diet drinks contain chemicals which have been shown in animal experiments to be carcinogenic – cancer causing.

Bulkers and Fat Blockers

Certain products are designed to keep you from absorbing some of the calories in sugar and starchy foods. In the early Eighties one well-known starch blocker in tablet form was made from raw kidney beans. Each pill was said to contain enough enzyme inhibitor to block the 'digestion and absorption of three to four ounces of starch' so you could eat pasta all day and get thinner. Sounds great. Except that taking these starch blockers leaves undigested food sitting in your colon to putrefy and create a lot of stomach trouble. Sugar blockers work by a similar method. Most contain an extract of *Gymnema sylvestre*, a plant from India, which its hawkers claim prevents sugar from being absorbed. Although chewing this plant does interfere with your ability to taste sweetness there is no scientific evidence that it either blocks the absorption of sugar or is helpful to weight loss in any other way.

Forms of free fibre, that is fibre which has been separated out from the food in which it is found, like glucomannan, xanthum and guar gum, as well as oat or wheat bran, are common ingredients in bulk-producing tablets that slimmers are counselled to take before a meal to curb appetite and create a feeling of fullness. There is no indication that using any of them has helped anybody shed fat. Glucomannan does not even bulk. As for guar gum, which forms a gel in the stomach, in some users it has created oesophageal obstructions severe enough to land them in hospital. Fibre is indeed essential for slimming but it is best eaten in its natural state – bound together in synergy with all the other nutrients in whole foods.

The bottom line is simple: slimming diets and appetite suppressants don't work long-term. They never have and they never will. There are five main ways in which they work to defeat even dedicated slimmers while helping the multi-billion slimming industry grow richer.

- They focus on shedding weight rather than getting rid of body fat.
- They reduce weight too fast which triggers the body's survival defences such as lipoprotein lipase and lowered BMR to slow down fat loss.
- They cannibalize your lean muscle tissue where fat burning takes place, lower your metabolism and decrease your ability to burn calories as energy – sometimes permanently.
- They hold out the promise of quick-fix solutions which ravage your health and looks long term.
- They make you feel more and more powerless with each bounce of the yo-yo.

Out of Control

The excitement of shedding a couple of kilos, followed by the dejection of the inevitable weight gain that follows, makes us feel more powerless – less in control of ourselves or our lives. So being lean and strong begins to seem a hopeless dream. Such feelings are common among slimmers, particularly women slimmers, who come to see themselves as inadequate failures in the face of continual bombardment from the media with its images of pencil-thin models with whom we are asked to compare ourselves. You are *not* the weak-willed, hopeless creature you may have feared (see Chapter 3).

So leave dejection and hopelessness behind and forgive yourself for whatever you perceive to be your 'failures'. To shed fat permanently you also need to decide that your strength, health and good looks *matter*. They matter not because you are *supposed* to be pencil-thin but because *you* matter. You are here on the planet to live your life fully and to become everything you can become. Growing lean is a process that will help support you in all of this.

There is only one kind of weight control which *does* work: the kind that allows you to eat your fill of satisfying wholesome food, protects lean muscle tissue and the body's water reserves, while it eliminates excess fat stores slowly and steadily. This kind of weight control also enhances your health and good looks, improves your metabolism and brings you lasting supplies of energy – regardless of age. Rest assured this is *not* an empty promise. It has been well tried and tested in leading-edge centres for the new lifestyle medicine and health education. Neither will it cost you a fortune in slimming foods and broken dreams. *Lean Revolution* is a way of eating and living that will not only help you grow leaner month by month but strong and clear, confident and in control of your own life. But to make it work, a *revolution* is called for. That is what this little book is all about.

ACTION PLAN
- Decide now to **Let Diets Die** forever.
- Forget about every slimming food and appetite suppressant you ever heard of.
- Stop counting calories.
- Decide that *you* matter. Commit yourself to doing whatever is in your power week-by-week to enhance your health and energy while you grow lean.
- Re-read this chapter once a week for the next three weeks.

Chapter Three

Tyranny of Commerce

One important question needs answering before we get into what *Lean Revolution* is all about: if our English-speaking world is so full of fatties despite all the money and effort we put into getting thin, how did we all get into this mess?

Widespread weight problems are a relatively new phenomenon. Obesity, adult-onset diabetes, kidney stones, hypertension, coronary heart disease and cancer of the bowel, together with many other chronic degenerative ailments, belong to a group of illnesses now known as 'Diseases of Western Civilization'. These conditions are hard to treat – so hard that, despite all the sophisticated drugs and leading-edge techniques of modern medicine, we have been unable to halt their spread. For, unlike the microbe-generated infectious diseases such as typhoid and tuberculosis, Western diseases are *lifestyle-caused*. Thanks to pioneering works from scientists such as Sir Robert McCarrison – who did the first studies on the relationship between diet and health – and Drs Weston Price, Denis Burkitt and Hugh Trowell, it is now widely accepted that being overweight and other degenerative conditions have developed as a direct result of the massive changes that have taken place over the last 150 years in how we live – especially in the way we eat.

Let's Go Back a Bit

A lot has happened to our foods in the last century to produce this state of affairs. First, they are *grown* differently from the way our ancestors for thousands of years grew theirs. We grow food on chemically fertilized soils in which the organic matter has been degraded or destroyed. Eating foods in this way leads to a depletion and imbalance in the minerals and trace elements available to our bodies – both of which we need in good quantities to support complex metabolic processes on which health and leanness depend. Secondly, our foods are now highly *processed*. Raw foodstuffs, instead of being made into meals in home kitchens as they were earlier this century, are sent to food manufacturers where they are fragmented – literally broken apart physically and chemically – then put through complex processes to alter them out of all recognition. Thirdly, our foods are shipped over long distances and stored for long periods of time, both of which lowers their nutritional value. These modern practices destroy a food's wholesomeness – a property very hard to measure except in terms of the degenerative effects that eating such foods has on our bodies. Destroy a food's wholesomeness and you destroy a food's ability to support the highest levels of health. And once the health-giving integrity of any food has gone it has gone for good. It can never be compensated for by vitamin and mineral supplements or by eating cereals to which extra fibre and vitamins have been added.

Our forebears, whether they were Africans, Indians, Orientals or Europeans, regardless of the staple foods they ate – rice, wheat, rye, barley, corn, cassava, yams or what have you – had two important things in common. Their meals were mostly prepared from foods of vegetable origin, and the foods they ate were little processed. They were *eaten whole, as closely as possible to their natural state.*

Such foods form the basis of a *Lean Revolution*. This kind of eating helps prevent the development of obesity

31

and other degenerative conditions, even if you happen to have inherited a tendency towards them. The even more exciting news is that studies carried out at leading universities and published in highly respected medical journals such as *The Lancet* and *The New England Journal of Medicine*, as well as clinical results from centres for health education and lifestyle medicine, now show that returning to what I call a *Go Primitive* way of eating can restore normal weight even to people who are very overweight. It can also free them from much suffering caused by degenerative conditions such as high blood pressure, arteriosclerosis, diabetes, and other Western diseases.

Food for Degeneration

The typical Western diet is based on 'foods of commerce' – the stuff you can buy at the local corner shop and in run-of-the-mill supermarkets. These foods are very different from the simple foods that human beings have eaten throughout history and to which our bodies have become genetically adapted. Our ancestors did not eat massive quantities of white bread, white sugar, junk fats and pre-packaged, pre-cooked foods like we do. They ate simple, ordinary, wholesome foods – as much of them as they could get. Their diet was *low* in fat, *high* in complex carbohydrates and only *moderate* in protein. Modern convenience foods are high in fat and depleted of natural fibre. They consist of highly refined carbohydrates like white bread and packaged cereals, spiked with lots of sugar and junk fats – that is oils which have been separated out from the foods in which they occur in nature then chemically altered by solvents and heat processing. We now consume masses of animal protein riddled with fat – milk, cheese, meat, eggs, fish and poultry. Even the leanest beef, pork or lamb is more than 50 per cent fat. Our ancestors didn't consume massive quantities of protein or high concentrations of fat – not in all history. As a result our bodies are genetically ill-equipped to

32

handle them. With a few rare exceptions such as the Eskimos and the Maasai, in all early cultures – the Chinese, the Greeks, the Indians, the Europeans, the Africans and the Egyptians – meat was used as a condiment or was eaten only on feast days – never every day. For several reasons – availability, cost or whatever – meat did not form the main part of a meal.

There is one more major change that has taken place: today we also swallow a kaleidoscope of chemical colorants, flavourings, additives and 'enhancers', not to mention pesticides, herbicides and fungicides, which our ancestors could not have imagined in their wildest dreams. We slurp down chemical pollutants with each sip of our diet cola and every bite of our pre-cooked meals. Such is the Western diet. So next time you upbraid yourself for what you perceive to be your lack of will power as you reach for yet another biscuit and feel guilty about it, let the guilt go. It does not belong to you. The denatured, degraded food we eat bears the lion's share of blame for the fat state we find ourselves in as well as for how hard it is in our culture to stay lean and to remain healthy.

Western Way of Death

It was Weston Price early on in the century who first brought the scientific community's attention to the devastating effects of the rise of processed convenience foods. Price, a dentist, travelled the world recording the changes in the shape of the jaw and teeth which take place slowly but inevitably as each culture discards its traditional dietary practices in favour of more 'civilized' Western fare. Price's many studies (each of which lasted between 20 and 40 years) carefully plot the onset of degenerative diseases including being overweight and obesity. It is not surprising that the human body, used to a diet of simple whole plant foods rich in natural fibre and the health-giving synergy of nutrients and micro-nutrients throughout evolution, should find the foods we now eat anathema to long-term health. Our genes have been attuned to Go Primitive eating for more than a million years. Our metabolic biochemistry as human beings is designed for it.

Many years after McCarrison and Price had completed their work, two British doctors Denis Burkitt and Hugh Trowell carried out their own extensive studies taking Price's work a step further. They carefully documented the exact sequence of events which takes place when a people's diet changes from primitive to convenience:

- *Stage One:* the primitive, unprocessed diet of plant eaters complete with large quantities of unprocessed carbohydrates and whole foods is eaten. There are very few examples of degenerative disease.
- *Stage Two:* Western diet is introduced. Obesity and diabetes become common among privileged groups able to afford foods of commerce.
- *Stage Three:* a culture's diet becomes moderately Westernized. Obesity becomes more widespread, as do constipation, haemorrhoids, varicose veins and appendicitis.
- *Stage Four:* Westernized diet now widespread. Being overweight and obesity are common in all social groups. So is heart disease, high blood pressure, diverticular disease, hiatus hernia, cancer and other Western diseases.

The degradation of our food has two major aspects, each of which is important to understand in depth. The first revolves around changes in the way food is grown. The second has come about from the way food is handled and processed.

Destruction is Two-faced

Early on in the twentieth century a few scientists – mostly in Germany – experimented with chemicals as a means of fertilizing food crops. They found that a mixture of nitrogen, phosphorus and potassium (NPK) would grow big-yield crops of good-looking vegetables, grains, legumes and fruits. But little interest was taken in their discoveries until the end of the Second World War. At that time most foods were still grown pretty much as they had always been – by farmers who manured, mulched and rotated their crops to keep soils rich and in good condition. To put it another way, most food was grown *organically*, although nobody had even coined the word, for this was no more than what farmers throughout the world had done for thousands of years. When the war ended, big chemical conglomerates who had been involved in the manufacture of phosphates and nitrates as war material found themselves stuck with huge stockpiles. They went looking for new markets.

Aware of the early research into chemical fertilizing, they turned towards farmers and began to sell them artificial NPK fertilizers at costs low enough to make it all look very attractive. These purveyors of chemicals also spread the false belief that NPK was all you needed to grow healthy crops. There were unfortunately two very important facts that the chemical hawkers left out. Probably they did not even understand these facts themselves. Maybe it was not so good for their profit margins to know. The first is that, although plants grow *big* on artificial fertilizers they do not *grow resistant to disease*. The second is that the health of human beings eating food plants grown this way can be seriously undermined.

Chemical Victims

Plants grown only on NPK are deprived of essential minerals and other micro-substances they need to synthesize natural complexes in roots and leaves which ward off attack by insects, weeds and animals. So, before long, the new artificially fertilized vegetables and fruits began to develop diseases. The chemical hawkers were quick to

35

the rescue. The answer to this problem, they said, would be found in using more chemicals. That is how pesticides, herbicides, nemacides and fungicides came into being. They provided chemical companies with yet another exciting business opportunity – especially since the longer you fertilize chemically the more depleted in organic matter your soils become – so that even if minerals and trace elements are there, they are not available to the plants because they are unable to synthesize natural protective complexes during growth – so the more pesticides you need. So, as time went on, more and more pesticides and other chemicals were sold. Yet, before long, another important fact began to raise its ugly head. It was this: like plants, human beings need a lot more than nitrogen, potassium and phosphorus from the foods they eat, to maintain their own health.

Your body cannot make minerals. It has to take them in, in a good balance, from the foods you eat. In addition to nitrogen, potassium and phosphorus, it requires magnesium, manganese and calcium, selenium, zinc, copper, iodine, boron, molybdenum, vanadium and probably other elements as yet undiscovered as well to stay healthy. These elements need to come from the foods you eat. Generally they do, when foods are grown organically in healthy, traditionally fertilized soils. But they are increasingly missing and unbalanced in the foods we buy today thanks to our legacy of chemical farming.

Go Organic

The organic matter in healthy soil is nature's factory for biological activity. It is built up as a result of the breakdown of vegetable and animal matter by the soil's natural 'residents' – worms, bacteria and other useful microorganisms. The presence of these creatures in the right quantity and type gives rise to physical, chemical and biological properties that create fertility in our soils and make plants grown on them highly resistant to disease.

When it comes to human health they do a lot more.

The minerals and trace elements we need to trigger the metabolic processes on which health and leanness depend must be in an organic form, that is taken from living things like plant or animal foods. You cannot eat nails – inorganic iron – for instance, and expect to protect yourself from anaemia, or chew sand – inorganic silica – and be sure to get enough silica (the trace element that keeps your nails and hair strong and beautiful, and helps protect your bones from osteoporosis). It is the organic matter in soils that enables plants grown on them to transform inorganic iron and silica into the organic form which we then eat, making these nutrients available to our bodies. Destroy the soil's organic matter through chemical farming and slowly but inexorably you destroy the health of people and animals living on foods grown on it. Organic methods of farming help protect against significant distortions in mineral balances – an increase in one or more mineral elements which can alter the availability of others. This can also undermine the people's health. No such protection is available when foods are chemically grown.

Hard to Cope

Your body has a remarkable ability to compensate for a mineral or trace element missing from your food. But, as a result of many years of our all eating nutritionally depleted foods, multiple deficiencies have become widespread. According to large-scale studies, few people in the West still receive all the minerals they need to ensure that the metabolic processes work adequately. And the deficiencies we are developing as well as the metabolic distortions that come in their wake – of which being overweight is only one – cannot easily be corrected. Popping the latest multi-mineral tablet from your local chemist or health-food store won't do it. For nutrients in foods exist in a complex synergy and affect each other.

37

They also interact and work together in your body. A balance of bio-available minerals and trace elements is infinitely more complex than vitamin fanatics would have us believe. To restore balance once it has been disturbed you need to return to good wholesome food – perhaps supplemented with extra green plants such as kelp, spirulina, chlorella, barley grass or alfalfa. This is a slow process taking months and even years.

Ostrich Syndrome

Our indiscriminate use of chemical pesticides, herbicides, insecticides and other chemicals has quite literally poisoned the land we live on and contributed to widespread obesity and degenerative diseases in other ways too. It was Rachel Carson, author of *Silent Spring* back in 1947, who warned that this would happen. She was viciously attacked for her brilliant book when it appeared. Chemical interests did everything in their power to discredit what she wrote. Yet now, half a century later, her prophetic words have turned out to be terrifyingly accurate. Since *Silent Spring*, many laws have been passed and many official agencies have been set up throughout the Western world designed to regulate the kind and quantity of chemicals used on the land. They vary greatly in their approach and powers from one country to another. But they all have one thing in common: an inability to stop or significantly alter the ubiquitous poisoning of land, people and animals.

The poisoning of our air, land and water continues to take place. In most countries it grows worse year by year. Like ostriches, we have tended to bury our heads in the sand and hope that what we don't see won't hurt us. Meanwhile, each year, more than one billion gallons of chemicals are sprayed on to crops. In the US 2.6 billion pounds of pesticides are spread over the soils – not to mention herbicides, chemical fertilizers, rodentocides and other chemical contaminants. Similar statistics –

from *official* government agencies – exist for every other English-speaking country in the world.

Poisoned Seals

In most English-speaking countries DDT was banned in the Seventies or Eighties. Yet in many areas its use still remains unchecked. After the ban, large stockpiles of the poison were sent to developing countries who had no limiting regulations against DDT. This is something we, in the so-called First World, do frequently. As soon as one chemical or another is put on our banned list we send it off to our cousins in developing counties for them to use. It is a practice not without sinister irony. For the cash crops on which they spread our rejects return to us in the form of sugar, coffee, tea and fruit which we then eat. Even in many countries where DDT is no longer to be found on the crops, it continues to poison marine animals and fish. Residues remain dangerously high in our own soils, the water, and in mother's milk. Meanwhile we have taken up newer pesticides which are even more toxic – dinoseb, for instance, and lindane, captan and alachlor – chemicals which controlled studies have already conclusively proven to be *carcinogenic*. We are still using them.

Chemical pollution not only does a great deal to harm the body, it specifically encourages weight problems. Whenever your body is exposed to poison in any form (from heavy metals such as lead or cadmium in air or water, or pesticides, herbicides and other contaminants in our foods), it makes big demands on the body's resources for detoxifying these pollutants. Enzymes such as glutathionine peroxidase and catalase, and anti-oxidant nutrients such as selenium and vitamins A, C, and E are needed in significant quantities. Your body's supply of these important enzymes and nutrients are also needed for many other functions of metabolism, including protecting your immune system. So when exposure is long enough and high enough then, as a means of

39

self-defence, your body will try to store such toxic residues as can't be adequately cleared away in a safe place. And that safe place turns out to be your least metabolically active tissues – the fat cells.

If you, like many of us, have inherited a propensity to gain weight, such body pollution only encourages you to grow fatter and fatter.

Fragmented Food

Like our soils, the industrially prepared foods of commerce we eat today have also quite literally been taken to pieces. High-tech food production works something like this. To create a great variety of palatable foods from raw materials you first have to reduce the foodstuffs – grains and seeds, vegetables and legumes – to simple, malleable 'nuts and bolts' that lend themselves to whatever manipulations you want to perform. Take soya beans. These little legumes contain a complete protein as valuable as meat or eggs – more valuable in many ways since it is so cheap. Food manufacturers take whole soya beans, in which 30 per cent of each bean is protein, and process them physically and chemically to extract this protein and make it ready to accept dyes and flavourings. They then alter its texture through more processing until eventually it becomes ersatz meat. This end product is a long way from the natural soya bean from which it was made.

In the course of such manipulations the little soya bean, once an excellent synergy of nutrients, complex carbohydrates, essential fatty acids and fibre, has now been turned into a highly concentrated artificial material. During the operation vitamins and minerals have also been destroyed and the soya bean's proteins and natural fatty acids have been denatured and chemically altered into new forms, some of which are not even usable by the body – except to lay down as fat stores. The soya has also lost most of its fibre – a vital part of a food's health-promoting wholeness and something absolutely essential

40

for protection from obesity and degenerative diseases. Its protein content has tripled and now approaches 90 per cent. To this artificial food, manufacturers then add a lot of phoney colours and flavours. Canadian expert in food science, Ross Hume Hall, puts it rather well: 'The product contains the same number of calories as the original soya protein, but it now consists of a set of naked molecules completely divorced from any natural context.'

From milk to meat to garden peas – whatever food is involved – processing destroys nutrients. According to official government handbooks, 50–70 per cent of vitamin B6 is lost when meats are processed. And 50–90 per cent of folic acid (a vitamin of particular importance to the functioning of nerves and the actions of hormones, especially in the female body) is shed when grains are milled while more that 80 per cent of the mineral magnesium disappears in the same process.

The multinational food industry, which tends to cover the packaging of its products with endless 'nutritional' information, would have you believe that any goodness lost in processing can be made up for by 'enriching'. Enriching is just another process whereby a few vitamins and minerals in synthetic form are pumped back into the now fragmented food. It is categorically impossible to restore the health-giving power of wholeness to any food that has been fragmented in this way.

Similar nutrient losses happen during other phases of food handling too – like artificial ripening, transport and storage. Store asparagus for a week and it loses 90 per cent of its vitamin C. Keep grapes for the same time and they shed 30 per cent of their B vitamins. Freeze meats and you can lose as much as 50% of two important B vitamins – riboflavin and thiamin. These are just a few examples of nutrient losses which occur every day. They are only the tip of the iceberg. Modern food handling and manufacturing processes create highly concentrated calorie-dense foods which are no longer able to support health. Neither can they protect those of us who have a genetic disposition towards gaining weight from getting fat.

Ask Any Rat

It is not just human beings who respond to processed foods in this way either. Studies show that when you feed rats on foods of commerce – what is commonly called a cafeteria diet – most of them get fat too. The more highly refined and processed the food you eat the hungrier you can become. There are many reasons for this. Because such foods are bereft of some essential nutrients, your body in its natural desire for them eats more and more. Also, continuing to eat foods 'constructed' from the same raw materials – things like milk, flour, corn oil and sugar – stresses your body's enzymes – all of which are food-specific. Because there is a particular enzyme needed to break down a particular food this can deplete your system of those enzymes and create food sensitivities – what are commonly and wrongly called food allergies – so that every time you eat something containing milk or flour you crave more. This is part of the bizarre but widespread phenomenon of chemical and food addiction. Another important reason for food craving is that the convenience foods are full of junk fats and sugar. The more you eat of either the more you want. After a couple of packaged biscuits, or a sloppy hamburger, or one of those chic and expensive packets of chicken drenched in wine sauce you crave more and more. Some foods are even sprayed with so-called flavour enhancers which encourage greed. Tinned dog foods fall into this category which is why dogs seem ravenous when they devour them. Foods that have been chemically grown, sprayed, treated and highly manipulated like this can never really satisfy hunger because they are nutritionally inadequate and chemically distorted. We can overlook this fact with our mind each time we feel a Big Mac craving coming on, but it is a truth our bodies know very well at the deepest levels.

Many overweight people blame themselves for compul-

sive eating and worry about their cravings for carbohydrates when they are caused by eating a high propor-
tion of foods from which the fibre has been removed.
Refining and processing strips our foods of their natural
fibre and in changing their physical form makes them
absorbed very quickly into the intestine. This is especially true of the average breakfast cereals and most of our
bread and biscuits, cookies and sweets. It is why you get a
slump of energy and hunger at 11 o'clock each day after
eating them. Such foods give only a temporary feeling of
having eaten enough. Very soon your stomach is back
again complaining of emptiness and demanding more.

Go Primitive

Dietary fibre is an integral part of every vegetable food as
it appears in nature. Fibre plays a central role both in
weight loss and in the successful maintenance of normal
weight. The naturally high-fibre Go Primitive diet of our
ancestors had a low caloric density. People eating this way
reach satiety far quicker than those munching away on
the products of the Western food industry with their
very *high* caloric density, devoid as they are of fibre and
stuffed with junk fats and hidden sugars. Eighty-five per
cent of the calories we eat in the Western world – animal
products, refined cereals, sugar, oils and fats – now come
from foods that lack fibre. The average person on a
Western diet gets only 10–25 grams of fibre a day. The
diet our ancestors ate and the more primitive diets of
developing countries contained between 35 and 60 grams
per day. So important is fibre in whole plant foods that
these facts alone would be enough to account for our
spreading waistlines. The bulky and moisture-rich foods
our ancestors ate – and which are still eaten in the few
primitive cultures that remain – are the foods from
which *Lean Revolution*'s Go Primitive menus are prepared.
Eat them and they make their full journey through your
digestive tract while neatly clearing away wastes and

43

toxins and decreasing the number of calories absorbed by the intestine.

Comfort Foods

Go Primitive foods are archetypal *comfort* foods. They are the kind of foods that make you feel deliciously satisfied. Rich wholesome breads, legumes, fresh vegetable stews, crunchy cereals and luscious natural sweets. They are foods in which the integrity of the components – natural proteins, fatty acids, fibre, minerals and vitamins – has been preserved. You will find they satisfy hunger as no other foods can since they are the kind of foods to which your body has been genetically adapted for hundreds of thousands of years. If you can get them in their organic form, so much better. If not, buy them as fresh as you can and incorporate special nutrient-rich items into your diet such as sprouted seeds and grains, seaweed or spirulina, chlorella or green barley.

In a world where much confusion abounds over how much of this and that you should or shouldn't eat, the simple Go Primitive diet is nothing short of revolutionary. For many, starting to eat this way is rather like coming home again. You begin to re-experience all the rich textures of real foods again with their wonderful aromas, colours and textures – all those things that our foods of commerce have lost and are continually trying to compensate for with the addition of chemical flavourings and colourings and bright seductive packaging. You may even find, as I have, that for the first time in years you enjoy cooking and food preparation again. For these natural raw materials – the crunchy grains, the colourful fresh vegetables and succulent fruits, the seeds and beans and nuts – can create meals that are as delicious as they are health-giving. Go Primitive. It is time to break free.

ACTION PLAN

- Right now forgive yourself for any past 'failures' in weight control. They are *not* your fault. You are not weak willed or hopeless. You have only been caught in a lose-lose scenario.
- Decide to explore the Go Primitive raw materials and begin to experiment with them. It is a whole new world.
- Go organic wherever possible when buying grains and legumes, vegetables and fruits.
- Find out more about pesticide control in your area and put pressure on the government to improve things.
- Stop buying highly processed foods.

Chapter Four

Come the Revolution

The *Lean Revolution* has two elements: nutrition and exercise. The Go Primitive diet is the nutritional side. It is based on what I call *real foods* – beans, fruits, vegetables, whole grains such as brown rice, wheat, rye, barley, millet, quinoa, leafy and root vegetables. A way of eating which is low in fats, refined starches and sugars, moderate in protein and rich in fibre, and high in complex carbohydrates from natural foods, it asks that as much as you can you choose foods grown on healthy soils and eat them as closely as possible to their natural state, either cooked or raw. Go Primitive is as different from the usual slimming diet as night from day. It is not a quick-fix solution but an invitation to energy, good looks and freedom from worry about weight control – for ever. Go Primitive is designed to help you to live longer and better while your body slowly and inexorably transforms its shape and composition towards sleek, firm muscles and away from soft or flabby flesh, regardless of age or how little or much fat you need to shed.

The second element of *Lean Revolution* is exercise. Body fat is only burnt within a crucible of muscle, in the presence of both carbohydrate and oxygen. The right kind of exercise for fat loss and permanent weight control both increases lean body mass by building and enhancing metabolism as well as bringing oxygen in good supply to the mitochondria of muscle cells where fat is burnt.

Metamorphose

Lean Revolution is a slow and completely transformative process – slow because it is organic, that is, regulated from within by your own individual metabolism. This makes shedding excess weight safe, effective and lasting. It is designed to dispose only of excess body fat while protecting your muscles and your body water. Such a process has to be slow so that your body is protected from cannibalizing its own muscle tissue and so that fat retention survival mechanisms are not triggered to defeat you in the accomplishment of your goal. Top expert in sports nutrition in the English-speaking world, Michael Colgan (who coined the word *fatpoint* and who understands as much as anyone I have ever met about weight control), insists that for permanent fat loss which spares muscle, protecting you from creeping flab, you must lose no more than 225 to 450 grams (½-1 pound) of fat per week. Adventists, doctors in America, and European experts in lifestyle health generally, place the figure a little higher, at 675 to 900 grams (1½-2 pounds) a week. But even they emphasize that *slower is better* – and more permanent.

Your fatpoint is the habitual amount of fat you carry in your body which hormonal messengers such as glyceryl rush to defend when you begin to lose weight. The fatpoint is neither permanent nor genetically fixed as many so-called experts in the past have claimed. It is *changeable*. Your fatpoint has shifted upwards gradually as you have gained weight. To shed fat without triggering defensive action, it needs to be shifted down again in the same *gradual* way. Says Colgan:

We have found that the *most* you can reduce your food intake to reset the fatpoint is 10% per day. Any

47

weight loss of more than half-a-pound per week is a warning that you are reducing too much. You will see little change for the first two months, but over a year, your fatpoint will edge downward by 3–6%. Meanwhile, your body is remodelling its adipose cells, hormones, enzymes, capillaries and other tissues to suit. In a year to eighteen months, you have reset the fatpoint without arousing a single bodily defense.

Go Primitive is primarily *vegan* – a vegetarian way of eating which excludes dairy products such as milk, cheese, yoghurt and eggs. This is because, like meat, all of these foods tend to be high in fat and fat is the one kind of food that you need very little of while getting rid of your own fat deposits. Go Primitive does not *have* to be vegetarian. If you feel you *must* eat dairy products, by all means have them – but *occasionally*, or in small quantities, instead of as big main courses. And choose any meats and fish you do eat wisely from ultra-lean, clean sources. Eat venison, for instance, or free-range boar, wild cod and coley instead of beef, lamb, farmed salmon and ordinary pork. Milk is second only to beef as the biggest source of saturated fat in the Western diet. Even low-fat milk, sometimes called '2% fat', boasts 38 per cent of its calories as fat. Cheeses and yoghurts follow suit. As far as milk products are concerned, learn to read labels carefully and, if you choose to eat them, only settle for products which have no more than 20 per cent of their calories in fat (see page 89 for how to calculate this).

Carbohydrate Works Best

Go Primitive is different from slimming diets in another way too. It does not limit the amount of food you eat. You will probably find that you are eating a lot more food than you are used to. For unless you get enough complex carbohydrates your body cannot burn fat properly. Go Primitive asks that you pay attention to the kind of foods you eat, however, that you consume the lion's share of your foods during the day when your body is most active and fat-burning intensified. It also asks that you drink a lot of water – probably a great deal more than you have ever drunk before.

KINDS OF CARBOHYDRATE IN VARIOUS TYPES OF FOOD

Food group	Percentage as sugar	Percentage as fibre	Percentage as digestible complex carbohydrate
Fruits	40–80%	10–30%	0–40%
Vegetables	10–80%	10–30%	0–80%
Beans	8–16%	20%	64–72%
Nuts and seeds	10–30%	20%	50–70%
Grains	0.5–2%	10%	90%

KINDS OF CARBOHYDRATE IN VARIOUS GRAINS

Grains	Total carbohydrate (g per 100g of food)	Percentage as sugar	Percentage as fibre	Percentage as digestible complex carbohydrate
Oats	67.0	0.6%	10%	89.4%
Whole wheat	72.0	0.6%	10%	89.4%
Popcorn	72.1	0.6%	10%	89.4%
Brown rice	77.4	0.4%	10%	89.6%
Average for grains	72.1	0.8%	10%	89.1%

Go Primitive has two phases. The first phase, Quickstart, is ultra-low in fat. It is designed specifically to be used during the period in which your body's excess fat deposits are being shed. During this phase only 10–15 per cent of your calories are taken in as fat. Quickstart has no cholesterol (unless you choose to eat small quantities of milk, eggs and meat products), is high in fibre, and excludes nuts, olives, avocados and all but the smallest quantities of high-fat seeds. This is because it is virtually impossible to achieve an input of only 10–15 per cent of your calories in fat if you eat too many of these foods. And to burn your fat stores you need low-fat foods. Research and clinical experience both in the United States and Europe show that on a Go Primitive diet of natural foods high in complex carbohydrates such as those recommended in Quickstart you will lose weight without calorie counting until you reach your ideal weight – for some people for the first time in their lives.

Although Go Primitive does not restrict your calories, most people using Quickstart, although they may eat twice the amount of food they have been used to, will actually consume far fewer calories than the average person on a typical Western diet. What is so difficult for most people embarking on their own Lean Revolution to understand is that you may actually need to eat a great deal more food that you have eaten before. For it is essential that your body be supplied with quantities of complex carbohydrates and that you don't go hungry. Complex carbohydrates are the energy foods which sustain you throughout the day and protect you from the hunger that defeats slimmers on calorie-restricted diets.

Never force yourself to eat but it is important that you allow yourself the freedom to explore the pleasure and satisfaction of these wonderful natural foods. Provided you chew thoroughly and give yourself time for meals your body itself will begin to tell you how much you need. If you do overeat for a while, fine. Don't worry. It is just you exploring your new sense of freedom with food. This is something I did at first out of sheer enthusiasm at being able to consume as much as I wanted of delicious peasant casseroles with thick slabs of Russian rye bread. It went on for about three weeks before I realized that by overeating I was decreasing my energy and I began to experiment with eating slightly less. I found I not only felt better but also enjoyed my foods even more. You may be surprised at just how much you will eat. I have always had a fairly healthy appetite. However, I have never eaten so much in my life as I do now on Go Primitive. Meanwhile the excess fat in my body continues to be shed month by month. Listen to what your body feels like and it will quite naturally help you to readjust your appetite.

What Kind Matters

Two recent studies, one at Harvard University and the other at Stanford University, have shown that in weight control the kind of food you eat is far more significant than how much food you consume. The Harvard study looked at 141 women between the ages of 34 and 59 and found there was virtually no relationship between how many calories they ate and body weight – even taking into account how much exercise they got, their age, and whether or not they were smokers and drinkers. What *was* directly related to their excess weight was the amount of fats – especially saturated fats – they consumed. The Stanford study came to the same conclusion, namely that the percentage of body fat that you carry is directly related to what portion of your daily calories come from fat rather than the total calorie intake. This is a major reason why Go Primitive Quickstart is ultra-low in fats.

Living Lean

Living Lean is the second phase of Go Primitive. It differs from Quickstart only in that it is more liberal in the use of natural high-fat foods such as avocados, olives, nuts and

51

seeds. It aims for no more than 25 per cent of your calories to be taken in fat. Living Lean is a permanent way of eating that will not only sustain your lean, firm body once it has emerged but – as clinical studies and epidemiological research now show – bring you and your family maximum protection from degenerative diseases such as coronary heart disease, arteriosclerosis, diabetes, premature ageing and various forms of cancer.

Both Quickstart and Living Lean have many things in common. They

- do not restrict calories.
- are low in fat and have virtually no cholesterol.
- exclude most if not all free-fats (the exception being a little olive oil or soya oil).
- are high in fibre.
- exclude caffeine and other stimulants.
- are based on real foods including whole fruits, vegetables, whole grains, green leafy vegetables, beans, legumes, herbs and root vegetables.
- exclude meat, fish and poultry, and milk products, except occasionally or in small quantities as condiments.
- exclude all refined and processed oils and margarines.
- exclude refined sugars and simple carbohydrates like white bread and most packaged cereals.
- discourage the use of alcohol except occasionally, at a level of less than two ounces of alcohol a day (two small glasses of wine or a small whisky).

In practice you don't need to worry about measuring fat and carbohydrate intake. The general outlines are all you need to worry about, the rest will take care of itself. You can stay on Quickstart for as long as you like. Many top athletes do because it's the best way to build muscle and to ensure that your lean-to-fat ratio stays high on the side of lean and low on the side of fat. But do keep an eye on your weight – it's important that you don't lose weight too quickly.

Let's take a look at how both phases of Go Primitive – Quickstart and Living Lean – compare with the typical Western diet that continues to undermine the health of hundreds of millions of people throughout the world. First, Go Primitive is a way of eating based mostly on complex carbohydrates – grains, vegetables, legumes and fruits. They are not only the best foods you can eat for energy and fat loss; they are, as research now shows, also the most protective foods in terms of guarding you against premature ageing. They provide your body with the continuous energy it needs to burn fat and supply the cleanest burning fuels for your cells. They are full of essential minerals, vitamins and dietary fibre, provided you take them in their natural form – brown rice, whole-grain breads and cereals and baked potatoes, as well as the legumes and pulses. Complex carbohydrate foods are very satisfying compared to the simple carbohydrates such as sugar, honey, alcohol, white flour and white bread which provide a lot of calories with little nutritional value. That is why on the typical Western diet it is easy to take in a great many calories without feeling satisfied or having any idea of just how many calories you are eating. University studies, such as those carried out by K. J. Acheson at the University of Lausanne in Switzerland, now show that it is much harder on Go Primitive for your body to convert the calories you eat into body fat. You also use up a great deal more caloric energy in digesting and metabolizing complex carbohydrates than you do in digesting and metabolizing fatty foods and simple carbohydrates.

Here are the most important things to remember about complex carbohydrates.

- They are your main source of energy.
- Eating a diet high in complex carbohydrates

protects your body's muscle stores from being cannibalized and lets your body use its fat as energy.

- 60–75 per cent of the calories you consume need to come from complex carbohydrates.
- The digestion of carbohydrates starts when food enters your mouth. If you don't chew well you don't digest carbohydrates properly and this can impede fat burning.
- When you eat a diet high in complex carbohydrates and low in fat (15–20 per cent fat) your blood sugar remains stable. You gain natural appetite control and emotional stability.

WESTERN DIET	QUICKSTART	LIVING LEAN
25–35% carbohydrate (simple)	70–75% carbohydrate (complex)	50–75% carbohydrate (complex)
25% protein	15–20% protein	15–20% protein
40–50% fat	10–15% fat	20–25% fat

In the average Western diet, 40–45 per cent of the calories are taken in fat, 15–20 per cent in protein, and 40–45 per cent in carbohydrates, most of which are simple – that is highly refined. There are very important reasons for this.

Excess Fats Cause Damage

Every gram of fat you eat has more than twice the calories of a gram of carbohydrate, and each fat calorie is harder to burn and easier to turn into body fat. Excess fat in your diet suffocates your cells, depriving them of oxygen, for too much fat in the blood causes the red blood cells to clump together and slows down the rate at which oxygen, needed for fat burning in the body, can reach the cells. This sludge in your blood lowers circulation by between 5 and 20 per cent and is the major reason why after a heavy Christmas dinner, rich in fat, you feel so exhausted and unable to think clearly. Too much fat in your blood also keeps your body from being able to metabolize sugars properly. High-fat foods also raise the level of cholesterol and uric acid in your tissues, paving the way for arteriosclerosis and gout. They also interfere with efficient carbohydrate metabolism and encourage blood-sugar disturbances that lead to diabetes and a pre-diabetic state. Finally, fats in meat, fish, dairy products, oils, margarines and butter are the foods which carry the highest concentrations of pollutants from pesticides and other chemicals. Eating those foods encourages the build-up of toxic wastes which seek a home in your own fat cells in an attempt to stay out of harm's way. There are only two essential fatty acids which you do need in small quantities – linolenic acid and linoleic acid. These will be provided by the Go Primitive staples – legumes, grains, vegetables and seeds (see page 90).

You will notice that Go Primitive is slightly lower in protein foods than the average Western fare. Recent research shows quite clearly that the body's need for protein has been greatly exaggerated for many years. There is strong evidence that eating excess protein can be harmful. Animals fed on a high protein diet grow more quickly and gain weight faster than the rest. But they also degenerate more quickly and die sooner. Eating too many concentrated protein foods is a major cause of the mineral loss in the bones that produces osteoporosis and promotes arteriosclerosis. Too much protein, eaten together with refined simple carbohydrates, can also raise blood-sugar levels and contributes to insulin resis-tance (see Chapter 5) which interferes with weight loss.

Go for the Best

You may be surprised to learn that the best sources of protein are not, as we have always been taught, animal products (sometimes called complete proteins) with all their hidden fats – meat, fish, poultry, eggs and milk products. It is now clear that the best protein comes from a mixture of vegetable foods – grains, roots, vegetables and beans, in their natural unprocessed form.

Proteins both from foods and in your body are made up of building blocks called amino acids of which there are 22 different kinds. When you eat foods containing proteins your body breaks these proteins down into their constituent amino acids and with them reconstructs whatever new protein it needs. Your body can make 13 of the 22 amino acids out of others. The rest – *essential* amino acids – you need to get from the foods you eat, but only three of them – methionine, tryptophan and lysine – are of any real concern since the rest are in great supply. Whether you get your proteins from animal foods or vegetable foods makes not one jot of difference. Although no single plant source apart from soya beans contains all the essential amino acids, a variety of plant foods will supply them all. Let me give you an example of what I mean.

Both grains and legumes contain most of the essential amino acids. Grains tend to be high in tryptophan and methionine but low in lysine. Beans on the other hand tend to be low in methionine and tryptophan but high in lysine. Therefore, if you have a piece or two of whole-grain toast or some whole-grain cereal for breakfast and at lunch a bowl of chilli, you will get all the amino acids your body needs to build its proteins in excellent balance, and without unwanted fat. On Go Primitive, making sure you get enough protein is something you do not have to think about at all as long as you eat some grains and some legumes during the day – ideally, approximately one-third legumes to two-thirds grains. You could eat tofu and rice, rye bread and black-eye peas with bran muffins for breakfast and lentil soup for lunch. There are a thousand ways of doing this (see the recipe section for some ideas to start you off). One hundred years ago in the West two-thirds of our proteins came from plant foods whereas now two-thirds come from animal foods.

What about milk and milk products? Believe it or not

milk is one of the foods highest in saturated fat that you will find despite the fact that on a carton of milk it will tell you it contains only 3.5 per cent fat. That is because this measurement is a percentage not of the total calories but of the total *weight* and since almost all milk is water, when you analyse milk you find that more than 50 per cent of its calories are fat. Even low-fat or semi-skimmed milk has almost 40 per cent of its calories as fat. The recipes for Go Primitive use soya milk. If you prefer cows' milk go for true skimmed milk. Even so-called low-fat milk is too fatty.

Eat Early

There are two more unique features to Go Primitive. First is the way your meals are distributed, for it reverses the time when the major bulk of your foods are eaten. Go Primitive asks that you eat breakfast like a king, lunch like a prince and supper like a pauper. Second is the way Go Primitive asks for periods of rest *between* meals. Clinical experience shows that not snacking or drinking anything except water between meals can improve digestion, help regulate blood sugar, and relieve the chronic hunger that so many slimmers wrestle with.

Scientific research has established that there is a strong relationship between a good breakfast and good health. In one study involving over 7,000 people carried out in the early Seventies in California, researchers found that men who skipped breakfast had a 40 per cent higher risk of dying than those who ate breakfast regularly. The risk for women was 30 per cent higher. This has recently been confirmed by another study involving 3,000 men and women. Skipping breakfast not only undermines stamina throughout the morning and decreases your motivation, it also impedes your ability to think clearly and can frequently result in irritability.

A good breakfast is a meal high in complex carbohydrates. Again, studies show that complex carbohydrate breakfasts create more energy, banish fatigue and encourage fat burning far better than a standard high-protein breakfast of bacon and eggs. Complex carbohydrates in whole-grain cereals, breads or beans help regulate blood-sugar levels for many hours after a meal is eaten. And a large meal early in the day brings your body the fuel it needs during periods of highest activity. Most important for weight loss, however, is that there is strong scientific evidence that the calories you take in early in the day are not laid down as fat in the body anywhere near as easily as the same calories eaten later.

One of the studies was carried out by the National Institute of Health. Researchers discovered that people who ate the same meal at 8 o'clock in the morning as others did at 5 o'clock in the evening lost 1½ kilos more per person in ten days. Equally important is that this weight came not from water or muscle loss but was drawn from body fat stores. In another study at the University of Minnesota people were put on a 2,000 calorie-a-day diet. At first they were given their allotment of calories at breakfast. Then the timing was reversed so that the calories were taken in the evening. All of the participants lost weight when calories were taken at breakfast. But the same meal eaten in the evening made two-thirds of them gain weight. The message is clear: *eat early to go lean.* In an interesting study of over 300 French school children, scientists discovered that those who skipped breakfast tended to be overweight while normal-weight children most often ate a good breakfast. During both Quickstart and Living Lean, Go Primitive asks that you eat a good breakfast. It should be the biggest meal of the day, eaten within two or three hours of getting up. Make lunch four and a half to five hours after that, your next largest meal of the day. And eat only a very light supper five hours or so after lunch, with nothing in between these meals except pure water.

Make the Change

For most people, the shift to eating a good-size breakfast, a moderate lunch and a very light meal at supper (perhaps only a piece of fruit and some toast) is quite a change. This is something that you need to do gradually. Like many people, you may feel you are never hungry at breakfast time. This is virtually always because of eating late in the evening or taking your biggest meal at night. It will change as you decrease the size of your evening meal. You must experience this yourself to be convinced of it. I did.

I have always been a very light eater at breakfast, partly out of habit but mostly because I have long been aware that the liver is most active between midnight and midday and therefore this is the best time for the body to detoxify itself. I did not want to put heavy food into my digestive system which might interfere with this process. What I didn't know, however, until I discovered Go Primitive is that on a diet high in complex carbohydrate and low in fat your body naturally detoxifies itself *all the time*. Neither did I realize that when you eat a large breakfast high in complex carbohydrate you begin to experience sustained levels of high energy all day long – quite apart from the fat-burning edge it brings. This is something I learnt from doctors at Loma Linda University. It is widely used in their revolutionary health education programmes with powerful results. Something else that I learnt from them is the importance of not eating between meals. Your digestive system, like the rest of the body, has certain circadian rhythms. Like you it, too, needs both work and rest. When you give it an opportunity to rest, not only does this help eliminate excess appetite – usually within a week or two – it also brings you even more energy.

These periods of rest don't often happen in modern life. We have become a civilization of 'grazers' who nibble on food or drink endless cups of tea or coffee, eating a biscuit or a piece of fruit, or some high-density snack like a bag of peanuts. Seldom do we go for more than two or three hours at a time without munching. Some of the health programmes based on complex carbohydrate natural foods urge people to eat as many as six or eight meals throughout the day. Fine for top athletes, maybe, who need to consume 4,000 or more calories a day but this is not good advice for anyone wanting to shed weight. If you eat too frequently you end up spending a lot of your time thinking about food or eating food – something which may already be an obsession. Also, when you eat frequently it continues to stimulate your digestive juices and confuses your sense of appetite. Frequent eating can also interfere with good digestion.

Eat and Rest

Studies carried out using X-ray to determine how long it takes a normal stomach to digest a meal fully show some fascinating results. The time needed is between four and five hours. In one study people were given what was considered an average breakfast of cereal, bread, cooked fruit and eggs. Then their stomachs were X-rayed. They were found to be empty again four and a half hours after finishing breakfast. The same people a few days later were given the same breakfast. But this time, two hours later, they were fed various snacks. Once again the empty-ing time was measured. The results were surprising. One person, given an ice-cream cone, was found to have the residue of his breakfast in his stomach six hours later. Another, given a glass of milk and a piece of pie, showed breakfast residue after nine hours. So did a third, offered a peanut butter sandwich. Two of the subjects were given repeated snacks. One ate half a slice of bread with butter every hour and a half throughout the day but took no dinner. Some of his breakfast was still sitting in his stom-ach undigested even nine hours later. Another was given a small amount of chocolate twice in the morning and twice in the afternoon. Half of his morning meal still lay undigested in his stomach 13½ hours after having eaten it. The body does not digest foods effectively and freely if you eat or drink anything but water in between meals. Even nibbling a handful of peanuts can delay digestion so much that eleven hours after breakfast there is still a large residue of your last meal sitting in your stomach.

Another study designed to test how quickly the stomach handles food was carried out on people who for one reason or another already had tubes inserted directly into their stomachs. After eating a meal their stomach contents again examined. Some were then given snacks between meals and their stomach contents were examined. Those who ate no more than three meals a day spaced wide apart, digested their meal. But those who had eaten every two hours or snacked between meals, at the end of the day were found to have part of their undigested breakfast sitting in the stomach along with some of the other meals they had eaten later in the day.

Every time we take new food into our mouth we stimulate our digestive juices. If we do this only a few hours after eating while our stomach is still engaged in the digestion of that meal, it is forced to turn its attention to the new food and begin the process all over again. It never gets a rest. Your stomach needs regular periods of rest for digestion is highly demanding work. If you do not give it enough time to clear all the food you have eaten before adding more, this can turn the process of digestion into a form of putrefaction that results in bad breath, lowered energy levels and poor health. Too frequent eating also causes disturbances which interfere with the messages of hunger or of satiety and make you think you are hungry when what you are really experiencing are digestive problems.

It is important for shedding excess fat that this should not happen for if the body's appetite centre, in the hypothalamus, has an error of as little as less than 1 per cent you will slowly and steadily gain weight year after year. Speaking about the appetite centre in the brain, one interesting fact is this: it takes twenty minutes after we begin eating before this appetite regulator can signal the stomach to turn off your sense of appetite. Eat too fast and you can easily swallow a lot more food than your body really wants. When you Go Primitive it is important to eat slowly and chew thoroughly. The flavour of foods comes to you through chewing. Chewing plays a very important part in satisfaction as well as in digestion. It makes all the difference in determining how much your body really wants to eat. If you don't chew well you can mistake appetite – a mental craving for food – for real hunger and over-eat. As far as digestion is concerned, chewing is particularly important when it comes to handling grains and cereals, beans and legumes. The digestion of these complex carbohydrates begins in the mouth. If they are not chewed thoroughly they will not be digested properly and you can end up with indigestion or flatulence.

Get the Edge

The real *pièce de résistance* of Go Primitive – that little extra push that makes all the difference to how smoothly and easily you shed excess fat in your body – is something I learned from Adventist doctors. I call it the Nightfast. For many centuries fasting has been used in controlled circumstances as an effective tool for cleansing the body and heightening mental and spiritual awareness. However, fasting in the ordinary sense should play no part in a weight-loss diet because of the effect that severe food restriction for long periods has on lowering metabolism and stimulating the production of the fat-storage enzyme, both of which undermine weight control. The Nightfast is different.

The fact is all of us fast every day of our lives although we seldom think about it. The word breakfast comes from 'break' and 'fast' – to break the period of not eating during the night while you sleep. *Lean Revolution* Nightfast only extends this fasting time back into the hours of the late afternoon and evening. Doing this can be enormously helpful in speeding effective weight loss without in any way slowing down metabolism. The idea of the Nightfast came out of late nineteenth and early twentieth-century traditions of natural health care and was part of American writer Ellen G. White's programme for improving health all round. Studies published as far back as a quarter of a century ago show that for many people eating two meals a day, provided the main meals are breakfast and lunch, and cutting out the third night meal, makes weight loss easy. Doctors report that patients who fail to lose weight when taking food several times a day can lose weight on the same number of calories when their meals are reduced to only two a day eaten earlier.

Pleasure and Privilege

Nightfasting is not something you want to initiate too early in your own *Lean Revolution*. It should be added only when you feel really comfortable about the transformation taking place in your body and are excited to explore it further. For it can be difficult for anyone who has been on and off restricted slimming diets and suffered the hunger pangs they bring at night to realize that not eating an evening meal can actually become a pleasure. However, once you are really satisfied on good, wholesome foods at breakfast and at lunch, you may find that you can easily cut out the evening meal and not suffer the slightest sense of deprivation. I find I sleep infinitely better without food in my stomach and awaken in the morning full of energy. I am able to take delight in a good hearty breakfast which provides me with energy throughout the morning and well into the afternoon. But be patient. The Nightfast is something each person has to come to on their own – something to be treated as a *privilege* – something to be experimented with and enjoyed once you feel ready for it. If you do not feel ready to give up the evening meal yet or if you are going out to dinner with friends, simply eat very lightly in the evening, some fruit and toast, or maybe some salad or a light soup. Before long you may be surprised to find that you enjoy eating more and more lightly at night. You will love the sense of not having your stomach stuffed with heavy food when it comes time to rest in the evenings, as well as having time free to do other things you enjoy, like exercise, reading, pursuing a hobby or spending time with friends.

Lean Road to Freedom

At the core of the *Lean Revolution* is freedom: freedom from ever having to worry again about weight control. Freedom to be what you are and not to have to conform to somebody else's ideas of what the perfect woman or man is meant to be. I value freedom greatly and would find it extremely difficult to feel free if someone were telling me what to do all the time. That is why you will not find long lists of do's and don'ts in the pages that follow. What you will find is an enormous variety of foods for you to experiment with so that you can discover which suit you best. Both phases of *Lean Revolution* – Quickstart and Living Lean – are designed to bring greater health and enjoyment to you and your family. It is my experience that when exposed to a wide variety of the wonderful real foods on which *Lean Revolution* eating is based, men, women and children come to love them. Both Quickstart and Living Lean are also excellent for athletes. The latest work in sports medicine shows that Go Primitive is unquestionably the way to go if you want to improve performance.

Deprivation and austerity do not belong in either phase of Go Primitive and it is important for you to realize that the odd binge should not significantly affect your own *Lean Revolution*. What you will be surprised to find is that the longer you experiment with Go Primitive foods and dishes, the less likely you are to binge at all. People often ask me 'How do you stay away from chocolate? Doesn't it take a lot of will power?' I am always surprised by the question. I *don't* stay away from chocolate. I like chocolate, but I don't feel a need to eat it continually. Like every other food, chocolate has its place and pleasures. I choose to eat the foods I eat day after day, first because I enjoy them. They have a more honest flavour and they are more satisfying than the others I have tried. I have experimented with a lot of foods and eaten a lot of pieces of chocolate cake in my life. In the process I have discovered that although I like it if it is well made, I also enjoy the way I feel when I don't eat it too often. When I do eat chocolate cake it is a great treat. Out of all this experimentation has come an interesting philosophy which I can't quantify through scientific research but which I find works very well indeed. It is this. Enjoy whatever you eat. If you are going to eat chocolate eat only the best chocolate. If you are going to drink wine, drink only the best wine. This goes for just about everything else you do. A little of the best has a real edge over lots of what is mediocre.

ACTION PLAN

- Begin to eat a good hearty breakfast.
- Decide to drink water between meals – lots of it.
- Explore the taste and textures of low-fat real foods by eating your fill of them without worrying about weight.
- Experiment with decreasing the size of your evening meal and see how it makes you feel.
- Read food labels carefully before you decide what to buy.

Chapter Five

Liberate Your Energy

The key to shedding excess fat is energy: you need to turn calories from the foods you eat and your fat stores into energy, while retaining your muscle tissue and body water. It sounds easy in principle. In practice it can be tricky. Calorie-restricted slimming diets don't do it. To understand what does you need to know a little more about your body's energy-handling processes. You also need to be sure about which kinds of foods to eat and which to avoid. Finally, you need to know how to protect yourself against blood-sugar problems and insulin resistance (more about this in a moment), both of which upset appetite-control mechanisms and prevent your fat stores from being burnt.

Energy Secrets

All energy production takes place within the mitochondria of your cells thanks to a process called the *Krebs Cycle*. The Krebs Cycle is your body's biochemical mechanism for turning food calories and fat stores into *adenosine triphosphate* (ATP) – the molecule which every cell uses as energy. Food is made up of three primary substances – proteins, carbohydrates and fats. In the stomach and small intestine these are broken down into building blocks – that eventually end up as molecules of hydrogen, carbon, oxygen and nitrogen – which are taken through the intestinal walls into the bloodstream to be carried to cells through-out your body. Once there, thanks to the Krebs Cycle, these molecules are transformed into ATP and stored. So when your body needs energy a molecule of ATP is broken down and energy is released. The Krebs Cycle lies at the core of metabolism. Through it everything you eat and drink – all those carbohydrates and fats and proteins – congregate to be burnt, stored, modified or recycled. It helps turn proteins, sugars and alcohol into water, carbon dioxide and ATP. It can transform protein into sugar or sugar into protein. It can also make fat from just about everything you take into your body except water and salt. If you could alter the Krebs Cycle's capacity for producing fat you would slow down the build-up of unwanted fat in your body and use up whatever excess fat stores you carry.

Happily there is a way to do just this – by encouraging the Krebs Cycle to change more of the calories you eat into water and into carbon dioxide which you exhale and excrete, and less into fat for storage. But to do this your body needs lots of oxygen.

Cells always have plenty of hydrogen but when oxygen is in short supply the broken-down products of food tend to combine with hydrogen instead of oxygen and form fats. Cattle farmers, aware of this effect, keep their animals as inactive as possible to fatten them up for market. Inactivity is the one thing you must avoid if you want to shed fat from your body. That's where exercise comes in. Exercise carries oxygen to all your cells. The more oxygen your cells receive, the more ATP they can produce. Regular exercise also increases the flow of adrenalin which in turn heightens your metabolism, bringing more heat to your cells for energy transformation.

Carbs are King

The kind of food you eat matters too. Carbohydrates are your body's main source of energy for all its functions, including fat burning. When you get enough complex carbohydrates this prevents your body from using muscle as a source of energy and lets it use stored body fat instead. The storage of carbohydrates takes place in the liver and the muscles in a form called glycogen. Carbohydrates are also kept in the blood stream as glucose or blood sugar. After you eat a meal, any extra carbohydrate is converted into glycogen and then stored in the muscles and the liver but once the capacity of both to hold glycogen is reached then any excess carbohydrates are either eliminated and/or stored as fat.

Studies show that the Krebs Cycle will burn fat most cleanly and efficiently *only* if you eat plenty of carbohydrate foods. The principle to remember is simple: *fat burns in the flame of carbohydrate.* Ideally you should get between 60 and 75 per cent of your calories from carbohydrates. If you do not supply your body with enough carbohydrates and enough oxygen it will not do its best to rid you of excess body fat. What happens instead is that you burn fat inefficiently, eat up your precious muscle tissue and create unwholesome by-products like ketone bodies. However, just any old carbohydrate won't do. Only *complex* carbohydrates will – lots of unrefined grains, legumes and vegetables which prevent your body from cannibalizing its own lean muscle tissue in an attempt to provide the Krebs Cycle with the raw materials needed to produce ATP. Complex carbohydrate both *spares muscle* tissue and brings *natural appetite control.*

Banish Sugar Bondage

One of the major weight-control problems caused by eating processed foods full of *simple* carbohydrates like white flour and sugar is that it brings about a progressive decline in your body's ability to metabolize sugar. Unlike real foods full of protective fibre, refined and processed foods are highly concentrated foods. Fibre is no longer present to dilute their concentration and to slow down the rate at which the simple starches and sugars they contain are absorbed into your bloodstream. Such foods are far more *calorie dense*. When you eat them year after year they begin to overwhelm the body – especially the pancreas – causing blood-sugar problems that wreak havoc with your health and encourage fat cells in your body to gorge themselves, swelling up as more and more fat gets stuffed into them.

Your pancreas, which sits inside the loop of the stomach under the spleen, is ivory in colour. It is a very special organ. Dr Warren Peters, director of the Centre for Health Promotion at Loma Linda University in California, refers to the pancreas as the 'princess' of the abdomen. 'She needs to be treated very carefully or she becomes angry,' he says. Your pancreas has two functions, an exocrine or *outer* function – which is to produce digestive enzymes to break down the foods you eat – and an endocrine or *inner* function to produce insulin which goes into general circulation in order to control blood-sugar levels and ensure that not too much of what you eat is taken up and stored in your body's fat cells. Insulin regulates sugar in your blood.

Eat a piece of whole-grain bread and your blood sugar goes up gradually. For the fibre and the natural synergy of nutrients in these foods enable them to be digested *slowly* releasing energy over a long period of time – over four or five hours. This produces a healthy blood-sugar curve which rises gently creating a steady release of energy so you don't experience tiredness slumps. It then tapers off just as gently several hours later when you are ready to eat again. This keeps the princess happy. But eat a slice of French bread spread with strawberry jam for breakfast and a cup of strong coffee and you have a different story.

Refined and highly concentrated convenience foods devoid of their natural fibre make your blood-sugar curve rise steeply as a lot of sugar is pumped quickly into your system, then drop off as quickly, so that after a couple of hours you get an energy slump and feel hungry again. It

69

is little wonder. Each teaspoon of sugar in the jam you eat is refined out of 1.8–3.6 metres of sugar cane and in the processing all the protective fibre and other nutrients, such as chromium, which your body needs for its proper assimilation, are lost. So a couple of hours after breakfast you have to reach for a bar of chocolate to keep going. If the snack you choose is, say, a couple of biscuits or a sweet roll you take in another 4 spoons of sugar – the sweetness of 9.6 metres of sugar cane – which you get in one big bang with no protective fibre to slow down its release into your blood. This jolts the princess pancreas who needs her beauty sleep, forcing her to respond quickly by producing more and more insulin to keep your blood sugar from going too high.

From Princess to Old Hag

Continue to eat concentrated processed foods year after year and your blood-glucose levels will tend to get higher and higher as the pancreas is continually forced to release more and more insulin in an attempt to control it all. After a while the fair princess turns into a burnt-out old hag and you have paved the road for obesity and an unending struggle with weight control. For even though insulin is still being produced in high concentrations your body will have become insulin resistant so that your cells no longer respond and the ability to control blood sugar is lost. When this happens, the calories from your foods are more and more easily converted into fats, or triglycerides, which are then laid down as fat stores on your belly, hips, thighs and bottom. You have also increased the likelihood of getting heart disease or other degenerative conditions for insulin resistance is a phenomenon linked to arteriosclerosis as well as adult-onset diabetes. Scientists once believed that this phenomenon was a normal part of ageing since it is now found everywhere in the Western world. Now we know different, for it does not occur in cultures living on a primitive diet of natural foods.

70

Natural Calorie Control

It is important not to eat more calories than your body can use. This is not something you need worry about since Go Primitive eating helps your body distinguish between real hunger and appetite by balancing the functions of metabolism quite naturally over time. Simple carbohydrates such as white sugar, white flour, cornflakes and white bread are *high* on what is known as the *glycemic index*. This means that they cause the blood-sugar level to rise quickly, contribute to insulin resistance, disturb appetite and make fat shedding difficult. It is better to choose natural foods which are lower on the glycemic index – such as apples, oats, brown rice, wholewheat spaghetti, lentils, sweet potatoes, lima beans and kidney beans as well as fruit sugar from apples and oranges. These are foods that you can feel comfortable about eating in quantity.

Meet the Glycemic Index

Don't get misled by the nonsense that is written on the packaging of foods you buy. Read the ingredients carefully and watch for hidden sugars which could interfere with the fat-burning process in your own body – glucose, sorbitol, invert sugar, corn syrup, maltodextrin, dextrose, barley syrup, malt sugar. Even many products which claim to be sugar-free contain one or more of these.

The beans and lentils, grains, vegetables and fruits of Go Primitive can save the day. Eating them helps stabilize blood sugar. Because these foods are high in fibre, real foods provide you with a steady stream of energy over many hours and prevent insulin resistance and extreme shifts in blood-sugar levels. The fibre they contain plays several other important roles in weight loss too.

More than Bran

To most people fibre means roughage or bulk. In recent

THE GLYCEMIC INDEX

100% (High)	80–90%	70–79%	60–69%	50–59%	40–49%	30–39%	20–29%	10–19% (Low)
Glucose	Cornflakes	Rice (white)	Bread (white)	Sweetcorn	Spaghetti (wholemeal)	Butter beans	Kidney beans	Soya beans
	Potatoes (instant mashed)	Weetabix	Rice (brown)	Digestive biscuits	Porridge oats	Haricot beans	Lentils	
	Maltose		Shredded Wheat	Rich Tea biscuits	Navy beans	Blackeye peas	Fructose (fruit sugar)	
	Honey		Bananas	Crisps	Peas (dried)	Chick peas		
			Raisins		Oranges	Apples		

A selection of foods, taken from Dr David Jenkins's Glycemic Index, which are particularly pertinent to weight loss.

years fibre has become a household word plastered over the brightly coloured boxes of so-called 'fibre-enriched' cereals. Talk about a high-fibre diet and people figure you are on about the F-Plan where a meal can consist of opening a tin of beans then slathering a slice of brown toast with them. But fibre is a lot more than that.

Dietary fibre refers to the components of plant cells and cell walls which are not broken down by digestive enzymes. It is by no means a single substance but many different components – cellulose and hemicellulose, pectin, lignins, gums, mucilages and the polysaccharides found in algae and seaweeds. Except for lignins all the components of fibre are polymers of carbohydrates – but carbohydrates that pass right through the body without yielding calories or energy. A specific plant food can contain several of these in differing proportions. A typical dry cell wall for instance can have 45 per cent polysaccharides, 35 per cent cellulose, 17 per cent of the woody lignins, 3 per cent protein and 2 per cent mineral ash. Each component exerts a different health-promoting and lean-preserving effect on your body.

Fibre was long believed to be something unessential in food and therefore happily discarded in the processing. Until, that is, Burkitt, Trowell and others showed that the consumption of unrefined high-fibre foods protects against obesity and the other Western diseases. Then everybody wanted to get in on the act. It does not take long for the commercial mind of the twentieth century to latch on to a winner and turn it into a quick-fix commercial product. So when the medical profession and the general public first became aware of the importance of fibre for good health this was often interpreted to mean that you could eat whatever you liked so long as you added an extra tablespoon of bran to your morning cereal. In fact wheat bran offers only one kind of fibre – insoluble fibre which can indeed play an important role.

Recent findings at the University of Pennsylvania and from Australian researchers, however, indicate that more and more people are unable to assimilate wheat bran when it has been separated out from the rest of the wheat and used as a supplement. They experience digestive upset and clogging. Using lots of wheat bran in this way can also bind vitamins and minerals and carry them out of the body before they can be absorbed, such as calcium, folic acid and iron. Get your fibre the Go Primitive way by eating a variety of real foods – beans and pulses, different grains such as millet, brown rice, barley, fruits and vegetables – and you never have to worry about this problem.

Easy Appetite Control

The fibre-rich foods of the Go Primitive Diet demand a great deal of chewing. This slows the rate at which they are eaten and stimulates the secretion of saliva and gastric juices so that your meal sits firm and full in the stomach and you are satisfied with fewer calories. Many have demonstrated that fibre-rich foods increase feelings of satiety and delay the onset of hunger for many hours. Eating real foods also increases the time it takes for them to get to the duodenum and decreases the rate at which starch is turned into sugar, which in time stabilizes blood sugar and sustains your energy. High-fibre foods (the complex carbohydrates) even alter brain chemistry in a way which helps stabilize emotions and brings a pervading sense of calm thanks to their effect on a brain chemical called serotonin.

The flatter the curve of your blood sugar, the easier it gets to shed weight and keep it off. Whole grains and legumes brimming with fibre complexes in natural balance, plus fruit and vegetables, bring you this full effect. It even matters how finely a grain has been ground as to how it affects the blood-sugar curve. Recent studies show that ground brown rice is digested more rapidly than whole brown rice, for instance, and triggers a greater blood-sugar/insulin reaction. Wheat bread made from

74

100 per cent of the wheat but from flour that has been ground very fine is also digested faster. Soft, mushy whole-grain breads can sometimes raise your blood sugar as high as white bread. So choose breads with lots of whole grains sticking out from them like the dark German pumpernickel or whole-grain rye, or make your own bread. A good rule of thumb is: the more processing a food has had, the less good it will be for stabilizing blood sugar, controlling appetite and sustaining energy for fat burning. Commercially tinned baked beans increase blood sugar and insulin levels far more than do home-made baked beans. Do not be fooled by 'granary' bread either. It is generally coloured white and mixed with grains of wheat.

Deep Cleansing

Fibre also helps keep your body clean. When wastes are allowed to build up in your system they can interfere with fat-burning energy production and also help to create false appetite. Natural high-fibre foods continually detoxify your body. The lignins in vegetables show anti-bacterial, anti-cancer and anti-fungal as well as anti-viral activities. The alginates in seaweeds, as well as pectin in fruits, help protect against absorbing damaging heavy metals such as lead or aluminium. They may even help eliminate them from the body. Oat bran has made the news thanks to its ability to lower serum-cholesterol levels. This fibre is particularly rich in beta-glucans – a water-soluble gum. The fibre in wheat bran boasts lots of cellulose and hemicellulose which are insoluble to water but *hydrophilic* which means they attract water. Both improve the function of the colon. Pectin and the bean gums also slow the time food takes to pass out of the stomach. They even help to eliminate fat from your system, enhancing the conversion of cholesterol by the liver into bile acids which are useful in the full digestion of fats and then help to bind these bile acids when they have finished their job so they are easily and safely eliminated from your body.

For optimal fat loss you need to get 30–50 grams of fibre a day. The table opposite gives you an idea of some good sources of fibre and what size serving of each contains 10 grams of fibre.

Plant Power

So important is preventing insulin resistance and stabilizing blood-sugar levels to fat burning and appetite control that if you can succeed alone in doing this you have won three-quarters of the battle towards permanent weight control. In my view, conventional slimming aids are of little use. There is one substance, however – truly unique in the world – which *can* help. Called Glycophos, its trade name is Glycosport, and it is designed to help athletes recycle ATP so that they can maintain steady energy reserves and enhance performance. Completely different to all other sports products on the market which tend to be sugar-based or made of polymerized glucose or glucose plus isotonic electrolyte fluids, Glycosport is a completely natural liquid which has been extensively tested by both amateur and professional sports people for five years. Taking a tablespoon of the product produces a measurable lift in blood sugar which begins within 15 to 20 minutes and lasts for four to six hours yet never overloads your body with bulk or calories – at only 18 calories per serving. Glycosport produces fifty times as much energy as the same amount of pure sugar without ever causing insulin resistance or a hypoglycemic rebound.

Glycosport is made through a process of biotechnology in which single-celled plants in purified water are fed on a liquid diet of phosphorus and glucose. These two substances become bound into the living plant structure in exactly the same way that minerals are taken up by vegetables grown in healthy organic soils, mimicking the

GOOD SOURCES OF FIBRE

FRUITS	weight	UNCOOKED GRAINS	weight	BEANS, PEAS LENTILS	weight
Dried apricots	40g	Buckwheat	100g	Butter bean	36g
Figs	50g	Popcorn	100g	Haricot beans	40g
Dried prunes	60g	Oats	100g	Kidney beans	40g
Nectarines	100g	Brown rice	230g	Mung beans	45g
Dates	114g	Barley	250g	Chick peas	55g
Blackcurrants	115g	Millet	300g	Lentils	85g
Raspberries	135g	Wheat	400g	Split peas	85g
Raisins	150g			Broad beans	160g
Bananas	300g			Adzuki beans	200g
Apples	400g				
Pears	400g				
Oranges	500g				

Note: Each quantity of food contains 10 grams of fibre.

natural process by which energy sources such as sugars are bound to the structures of complex carbohydrate foods. The plants are then sacrificed to break down the cell walls and what remains is Glycosport.

Chemically, Glycosport is a monosaccharide linked to the element phosphorus. It contains complex polysaccharide glycosides and phosphorus – important in the conversion of ATP into energy – incorporated within active sugar molecules which allow blood-sugar levels to build in a unique way. No one understands exactly how Glycosport works. Dr David Smallbone, an expert in biochemistry who has worked with the substance for several years, says:

I believe the action of Glycosport is multi-faceted. This accounts for its apparent broad spectrum of activity. It probably mobilizes energy into the blood supply in a gradual way, through many different means, such as the conversion of liver and muscle glycogen stores – a process called glycolysis, the release of energy from the burning of fat reserves, and by stimulating the production of ATP recycling the breakdown products of energy use. It may be many years before we fully understand the remarkable action that Glycosport has on the body but one thing is sure, there is nothing like this effect to be found from any other known material. Only recently has it been discovered that Glycosport is a great aid for weight loss. At the four Diet UK clinics in Britain, doctors now use it as a central part of their weight management and weight-loss programmes. Without ever having to rely on severe calorie restriction they report excellent results. Director of the clinics, Dr Sindy Butoo, who has been using the product for a year, gives her patients 10–15 ml once or twice a day – 15 ml is the equivalent of a tablespoon. She has found it aids weight loss and fat burning in three major ways:

- It regularizes blood sugar and eliminates energy slumps.
- It helps get rid of cravings associated with binge eating.
- It creates energy for the slimmer and encourages him or her to get regular exercise.

Other doctors using Glycosport claim they too have been able to reduce the use of appetite suppressant drugs dramatically. Glycosport also has a remarkably positive effect on pre-menstrual syndrome. 'Increasing the dose to 30 mls a day during the pre-menstrual period, it curbs sugar craving and banishes tiredness,' says Dr Butoo. 'We have never come across anything like Glycosport. It seems to support the body's own biochemistry, helping it to regulate energy, appetite and mood. We have now given it to a thousand people. I am surprised and delighted with the positive clinical results.'

Glycosport (or Glycoslim which is virtually the same product) is unquestionably the most useful tool for natural weight loss that I have ever come across. It is taken in doses of 10–15 ml once or twice a day half an hour before the onset of your lowest energy levels – 11 o'clock in the morning and 4 o'clock in the afternoon for most people. The only negative thing about Glycosport is that, because it is a completely natural product and has nothing added to it in the way of flavourings or colourings, it has an extremely strong, earthy taste. This is easily masked in a small amount of grapefruit juice or orange juice.

As you instigate a *Lean Revolution* in your own life you will find that appetite control and fat burning begin to happen of their own accord. Week by week your sense of trust in your own body's capacity for regeneration grows and past anxiety about weight loss begins to fall away as slowly, organically, your body transforms itself. The sense of relief that this brings can be quite remarkable. Not only do you find yourself with energy you never dreamed you had, you can experience a profound sense of freedom – freedom to let go of worry about weight control and leave the responsibility in the hands of your body's natural metabolic processes.

ACTION PLAN

- Take pity on your princess pancreas – steer clear of *simple* carbohydrates – white flour and sugar.
- Eat plenty of *complex* carbohydrates – grains, beans, lentils, fruits and vegetables to do away with sweet cravings and snacking.
- Throw out all those 'fibre-enriched' breakfast cereals.
- Try to take in 40 grams of fibre a day from real foods – keep referring to the fibre chart.
- Consider adding Glycosport or Glycoslim to your *Lean Revolution* programme taken once or twice a day.

Chapter Six

Fatty Acid Charter

The Western diet of convenience foods high in fat is a perfect way of turning a power person into a wimp. Studies reported recently in the *British Medical Journal* show that both people and animals on a low-fat diet are significantly more independent and self-assertive than those living on high-fat fare. Low-fat eating increases energy and strength – something that I have noticed in myself since adopting Go Primitive. So have many athletes I know who have done the same. An important part of the whole experience of *Lean Revolution* is the way it taps you into a new sense of personal power and confidence. The exact biochemistry of how this happens is still not completely understood. Part of it certainly has to do with increased oxygen levels to the cells all over your body, including your brain. Also, when you eat a diet in which only 10–15 per cent of your calories come from fat (provided, of course, you get enough *essential* fatty acids which act as energy carriers at a molecular level), you feel altogether more alive.

Fat Calories are Fatter

One of the biggest lies that purveyors of slimming diets spread is that it doesn't matter where your calories come from so long as you eat a certain number. Impeccable research shows this to be absolutely untrue. Fat calories are fatter than lean calories. To shed body fat you must reduce your daily intake of fat from foods. Numerous studies on humans and animals show that you put on a lot more body weight by eating fat than by eating the same number of protein or carbohydrate calories. At the University of Illinois, Dr Wayne Miller and his colleagues carried out some interesting studies on rats. To one group they fed a diet which, like a Western diet, took in 42 per cent of its calories from fats. To another they fed low-fat foods based on whole grains. They let the rats in both groups eat as much as they wanted. After 60 weeks the high-fat group had ballooned up like butter balls and they had an average body-fat level of 51 per cent. The low-fat group remained lean and sleek.

Studies also show that how easily you gain weight depends to a large degree on the *kind* of fat you eat. Unsaturated fats, from grains and legumes, seeds and nuts, are oxidized by the body for energy far more easily than saturated fats from animal foods like cheese and meat which tuck themselves too readily into your fat cells, like long-term deposits in the bank. While it is true that your body can convert both carbohydrates and proteins into fat – should you happen to eat too much of either – this conversion uses a lot of energy. It takes 2 grams of excess protein or carbohydrate to produce 1 gram of fat and you burn calories in the process. But the calories from the fat you eat are laid down as fat stores easy as pie with little energy burnt. You would have to gorge on carbohydrates and protein to lay down fat, whereas every fat calorie that you eat finds its way to your hips with ease.

Forget Fat-free

Even so, Go Primitive is *not* a fat-free diet – for very important reasons. Despite its beneficial, temporary effects on overall health, the fat-free diet, which first became popular in the Seventies and Eighties (mostly as a result of the revolutionary work reversing degenerative diseases that Nathan Pritiken did in California), has not turned out to be as efficacious for permanent weight loss as was first hoped. The first clinicians using it got the general basis right, but remained largely unaware of the vital role that specific fatty acids themselves can play in shedding body fat. After the first three or four months on a fat-free diet, many people begin to feel hungry all the time, no matter how much food they eat – probably because fatty-acid deficiencies are beginning to surface as a longing for fat foods. In some people immuno-suppressive difficulties such as viruses, multiple-food allergies and chemical sensitivities develop when they eat fat-free. For essential fatty acids play a central role in immunity. The fat issue is highly complex. Let's take a look at how fat fits into a *Lean Revolution* as well as what kind of fat to seek and what to avoid.

Each of us in the West consume about 175 grams of fat a day. That makes 63 kilograms a year since between 40 and 50 per cent of our food calories come from fat. The biscuits you buy in your local supermarket are well over 40 per cent fat and the munchy-crunchy snacks which masquerade as 'health bars' seldom contain less than 50 per cent. Go Primitive helps you reduce your fat intake down to 10 or 15 per cent of the calories you eat while shedding flab. Afterwards, when you are Living Lean, you can be more liberal and eat up to 20 per cent or even 25 per cent of your calories in fat. Both phases of Go Primitive ask, however, that you take great care to make sure that these fat calories are the right kind. This is not always easy to do.

All Fats Are Not Equal

All fats and oils in our foods are made out of fatty acids. A fatty acid is a molecule that contains an acid part and a fat part. Chemically it consists of a chain of carbon and hydrogen atoms to which one oxygen atom is attached. A molecule of fat differs from a molecule of carbohydrate (which also is made out of carbon, hydrogen and oxygen) by the fact that the fat contains a lot less oxygen. This makes it highly concentrated and is why there are 9 calories in each gram of fat while only four calories in each gram of carbohydrate or protein. Fattyacid chains come in many lengths. Some, such as caproic acid, found in cheese, has only 6 carbon atoms, or acetic acid in vinegar has only 2. They are called the shortchain fatty acids. Others, such as those you find in the human brain and in some fish oils, contain as many as 20–24 carbon atoms to each molecule. These are known as the long-chain fatty acids.

Fats can be roughly divided into two groups – saturated and unsaturated. A saturated fat is a fatty acid with a molecule where each carbon atom is connected to a hydrogen atom so that there are no empty *spaces* to allow one or more of the carbons to reach up and join together with molecules of other substances in your body. Because of this, saturated fats (found in meat, dairy products like cheese, ice-cream, milk and the tropical oils like palm kernel oil and coconut) are stable, inactive and virtually inert in your body. Their only *raison d'être* is to provide calories in a concentrated form which can later be burned as energy. Eat foods full of saturated fats and they do their best to lay themselves down as fat stores. Saturated fats play no other part in keeping your body healthy. You will get as much saturated fat as you need from your food without ever giving it a second thought. Saturated fats are not 'friendly' fats when it comes to losing weight. So make an effort to steer clear of foods containing them.

Saturated vs Unsaturated

Unsaturated fats are different. They are made up of fattyacid chains which *do* have empty spaces – carbon atoms with open arms which are not connected directly to hydrogen atoms. Unsaturates come in two forms: *mono*unsaturates like olive oil and *poly*unsaturates, found in corn, sunflower seeds, peanuts and many other foods from which they are extracted. Thanks to their free spaces, monounsaturates and polyunsaturates are much more biologically active – more able easily to take part in important biochemical changes in your body that produce energy, create hormones and help burn stored body fats. That is the right *kind* of unsaturated fat.

There is a lot of hokum spread about unsaturated fats by sellers of margarine and producers of processed junk foods. Just because a label says 'unsaturated' it doesn't mean the food in the packet is good for you. Ninety-eight per cent of them won't be. You have to be shrewd about what you buy and really know the ropes. This means going a bit deeper into the whole fat issue. But bear with me. A good understanding of good and bad fats can revolutionize your health and good looks.

Essential Friends

Your body can make all the fat it needs for daily metabolic processes except for two essential fatty acids, linoleic and linolenic – more about these in a moment. They are found naturally in fresh foods – in seeds and nuts, in vegetables and fish – even in wild meat such as game. For optimum health you need no more than 2–4 tablespoons of these essential fatty acids a day yet, despite our high fat intake in the West, they can be as hard to find in modern convenience foods as the proverbial hen's teeth.

These two unsaturates play a vital role. They help you burn body fat and build energy. Linoleic and linolenic are called essential fatty acids because that is exactly what they are – essential to human life and health. Important for your brain and nerve cells, your skin and hair, they also form the building blocks for cell membranes all over your body. When you get enough of both in good balance your skin holds water well, making it smooth and young looking, and just about every biochemical process in your body functions better. They are precursors to highly reactive local hormones called prostaglandins which you need to make many of your metabolic processes turn over.

The problem with linoleic and linolenic acids (both of which are unsaturated fats) is that the chemical reactivity which gives them their health-giving power also makes them highly unstable so they spoil easily and are easily damaged. Natural foods that contain them such as grains and seeds will turn rancid in contact with air since unsaturated fats oxidize rapidly, although their rancidity may not be noticeable by taste or smell.

Beware of Free-fats

The moment you remove an unsaturated fat from the food in which it comes you produce what is known as a *free-fat*. A free-fat is any fat which has been separated out from the food in which it occurs in nature – corn oil for instance, peanut or groundnut oil, sunflower oil, safflower oil and all the rest, as well as any margarines or biscuits or other foods containing them. Free-fats are something to avoid like the plague. You need to get your fats the way they come, packaged by nature in fresh real foods, complete with all the protective fibre, anti-oxidant vitamins such as vitamin E and minerals. For through complex operations involving the use of heat and unpleasant chemical solvents, food manufacturers turn our natural fatty acids into highly artificial fat products which can damage our health and impede weight loss. It takes an amazing 12–15 ears of corn to produce a mere dessertspoon full of the golden oil, while all that protective packaging gets thrown out or fed to pigs. Advertisers are continually promoting their products as full of 'polyunsaturates' as though they were healthy. It is a lot of rubbish. Most polyunsaturated fats are not at all healthy. Let me give you an example of what I mean. In addition to the common process of 'hydrogenation' which turns an unsaturated fat into a saturated one, making an oil into a solid fat like margarine by adding extra hydrogen atoms to spaces on the fatty-acid chain, there are other processes commonly used in food processing which degrade or completely destroy the health-giving properties of whatever essential fatty acids a polyunsaturated fat may contain.

Natural, unadulterated, unsaturated fats needed for health come in a chemical configuration known as a *cis* form. This is the *only* form that your body can use for anything except pumping up its fat stores. Cis fatty acids are destroyed by modern processing procedures such as bleaching, hydrogenation, heating and deodorizing – procedures that turn out the golden oils that shimmer from the shelves of our supermarkets and with which the mass-produced foods we eat today are riddled. These procedures change our healthy cis fatty acids into unhealthy *trans* fatty acids by rotating the hydrogen atoms on the fat molecules so that they change sides. Cis fatty acids – the good guys – are rather like 'gloves'. They fit perfectly on to the 'hands' of the molecular fat receptors in your body. Trans fatty acids are bad guys. They not only don't fit hand-in-glove into your body's metabolic machinery, but their presence in your body helps to make you fatter and actually helps to gum up the whole works.

Bad Guy Fats

Since trans fatty acids don't occur in nature your body has never developed any mechanisms for making use of them. Instead, it treats them as foreign invaders rather like toxic waste and does its best to try to protect you from any detrimental effects they can have on your body, such as furring up your arteries, by laying them down in fat tissues. This is why a first principle of the *Lean Revolution* is *eliminate free oils, hydrogenated fats and processed foods from your diet.*

Every processed fat contains these unhealthy trans

fatty acids. Not one mass-produced margarine on the market is genuinely health-promoting despite all the advertising designed to convince us to the contrary. Nor are all those golden oils, salad dressings and biscuits, breads or ready-made meals which contain them. So don't be misled by the words 'contains polyunsaturates'. Margarines and cooking oils are junk fats. Your body cannot use them for health and their presence actually blocks the uptake of cis fatty acids in your diet and can lead to fatty acid deficiencies. Even the ordinary saturated fat that you find in steak or chicken is healthier than such artificially produced, hydrogenated, unnatural fatty acids. It is important for *Lean Revolution* shopping that you read every label and anything that says it contains hydrogenated vegetable oil or partially hydrogenated vegetable oil leave on the shelf.

Beware of Fat Frauds

But don't assume you can believe everything you read on food labels either. Many of the so-called 'lite' foods are not light at all, they are full of junk fats – 'lite' burgers, for instance, or 'lite' chicken chunks in fast food restaurants from which the skin has been removed. The only thing 'light' about them is that they don't weigh as much as normal chicken chunks. As far as many of the low-fat or fat-free salad dressings and margarines are concerned, most come nowhere near the low-fat demands of the Go Primitive diet, and if you read the labels carefully you will often find many are lower in fat simply because the serving size listed on the label is smaller than an ordinary serving of salad dressing or mayonnaise. So long as you are cooking your foods from scratch, that is grains and pulses, fruits and vegetables, you don't have to worry about fat content provided you are not eating huge quantities of avocados or nuts. When you go searching for ready-made foods you have to be very careful indeed. Even many of the so-called low-fat biscuits have a lot of hidden oils and boast 45–50 per cent of their calories in fats. Crisp breads are pretty good but again read labels carefully and don't buy anything that has more than 20 per cent of its calories in fat.

Check Out Fat Calories

Look on any packet of milk, cheese, biscuits, breads or what-have-you, that lists the protein, carbohydrate and fat content, and the calories per serving, and make some quick calculations to tell you what percentage of the calories in the food are fat calories. Here's how to work it out quickly. Say a particular packet of biscuits contains 145 calories per 100 g serving, which includes 4 grams of protein, 19 grams of carbohydrate and 7 grams of fat. Multiply the amount of fat by 10 (rounded up from fat being 9 calories per gram), i.e. add a zero to the number of grams of fat per serving to give you how many of the calories per serving are in the form of fat. Then compare this figure with the total calories. In this case it would be 7 x 10 = 70 calories of fat in each 145 calories. Now divide 70 by 145 and you get 0.48 – the percentage of those calories per serving which come from fat. In other words, this tells you the biscuits are about 48 per cent fat. As this is way above the Go Primitive limit of 15 per cent for Quickstart and 25 per cent for Living Lean, reject the packet. As far as the golden vegetable oils that you find on supermarket shelves are concerned, don't use them. On your salads, instead of using salad oils, explore some of the recipes for low-fat dressings or use a teaspoon or so of *cold pressed extra virgin* olive oil. This oil is not a polyunsaturate with many free spaces on its molecules, but a monounsaturate with only one free space which makes it highly stable. It is the best overall oil for salads. You can also use it in tiny quantities for wok-frying vegetables.

So just where do you get the important unadulterated essential fatty acids that you need for turning your body lean and how do they work? The answer to the first question is simple. Essential fatty acids are found in abundance in nuts, beans, grains and seeds, as well as in olives and other plant foods. With the exception of avocados, nuts and olives, most of these whole plant foods have a low-fat content perfect for the *Lean Revolution*. Animal foods, however, have a much higher fat content. Even the leanest steak boasts 50 per cent of its calories from fat while the more delicious fat-marbled variety can be as high as 80 per cent. Butter and cream go even higher, offering 100 per cent of calories from saturated fats, none of which you need for health and all of which work against you developing a lean body:

FAT CONTENT OF VARIOUS TYPES OF FOOD

Food group	Fat content
Grains, beans, fruits and vegetables	0–15%
Low-fat fish	0–30%
Fatty fish (e.g trout, mackerel, salmon)	50–60%
Milk	50%
Eggs and cheese	60–80%
Meat	60–85%

The Go Primitive foods will automatically supply your body with the 15 per cent of essential fatty acids that it needs. Soya beans, for instance, are an excellent source, so are grains like wheat and barley, oats and maize. What happens in your body when you eat these foods is that the linoleic and alpha-linolenic acid they contain are converted into other fatty acids that are needed for various purposes, provided, of course, that your diet is not full of junk fats that prevent these conversions from taking place. It is important to buy your foods really fresh. Reject any grain or seed or nut which does not taste and smell absolutely clean and keep your nuts and seeds in the fridge.

Clever Conversions

In your body linoleic acid is converted by an enzyme called the delta-six-desaturase enzyme into gamma-linolenic acid, or GLA, which these days has become well known as a way of improving the skin and as a treatment for a number of female problems such as PMT. GLA is in turn changed into prostaglandins and different fatty acids such as arachidonic via other metabolic steps. Linolenic, the other essential fatty acid, is present in pumpkin seeds, flax seeds, soy beans and walnuts, as well as in oily fish such as wild salmon, mackerel, sardines and wild trout. Because of the way they are fed these days, farmed fish such as trout and salmon contain more and more saturated fat and less and less linolenic acid. Linolenic is similarly converted through the action of an enzyme called delta-five-desaturase into eicosapentanoic (EPA) and then into docosahexanoic acid (DHA).

A major reason why GLA from evening primrose oil has such a positive effect on the body is that because our Western diet is high in junk fats or trans fatty acids we often have difficulty making the conversion from linoleic to gamma-linolenic. Similarly, in recent years, fish oils containing EPA and DHA have been prescribed particularly for athletes, slimmers and people at risk from heart disease because as we get older there appears to be a decline in the enzymes that are necessary to make these conversions. So important are these essential fatty acids and the conversions which your body makes from them that many leading-edge researchers and clinicians now believe that in addition to the essential fatty acids you naturally get when you Go Primitive, they can offer extra help in eliminating the stores of hard fats on the hips and tummies of overweight people and have begun to prescribe them in small extra doses as nutritional supplements.

Extra Helpers

Experts in sports medicine often use them too. Michael Colgan, at the Colgan Institute in California, recommends that his older athletes take extra GLA either from evening primrose oil or borage seeds. Similarly, he uses EPA and DHA derived from fish. Much recent research shows that they help prevent the development of insulin resistance and blood-sugar problems. At the Garvin Institute of Medical Research in New South Wales in Australia, scientists have discovered that when you supplement an animal's diet with fish oils containing EPA and DHA they never develop the kind of disorders of insulin metabolism that other animals do even when fed on the high-sugar, high-fat diet that we eat in the West. One way of getting extra quantities of essential fatty acids is to buy vacuum-packed flax seeds, pulverize them and sprinkle a dessertspoonful or two on your cereals or salads every day.

The oil found in flax seed or linseed is an almost perfect balance of linoleic and linolenic acid. Linoleic acid is prominent in many vegetables. Linolenic acid belongs to the Omega 6 family. These are the fatty acids which are most prevalent in fatty fishes. What makes flaxseed oil so exceptional is that it has such a high degree of the Omega 3 fatty acids which are particularly important in fat burning. I grind flax seed in a coffee grinder and then put it into a tightly covered jar and store it in the refrigerator. I use 2–4 dessertspoons a day. It is important to go for the very best German vacuum-packed linseeds, however, in order to make sure that the precious fatty acids which they contain are protected from rancidity (see Resources p.185). It is as easy as that to make sure you get all the essential fatty acids provided you steer clear of junk fats and processed oils. Your body will do the rest.

During the Quickstart phase of Go Primitive you will want to keep your total fat intake to around 10–15 per cent of your daily calories. This means 1 dessertspoon of olive oil and a couple of flaxseed oil a day as well as perhaps a small pat of nut or seed butter spread on your bread. Once your *Lean Revolution* is well on its way you can be more liberal and go up to 20 per cent or even 25 per cent while Living Lean. If you are not a vegetarian and you are eating a couple of meals a week of cold-water fish then you are likely to be getting all that you need of the essential fatty acids to support your fat-loss process. If you are a vegetarian it is a good idea to increase the flax seeds that you are taking. If you are aged over 35 you might also consider taking some extra GLA as well as the fish oils EPA and DHA for extra support – see Resources for the best – especially if, like me, you enjoy exercise and get a lot of it. Consult a nutritionally aware doctor about your needs or read up on fats in Colgan's book *Optimum Sports Nutrition* (see p.188). It is the best book I have ever come across on nutrition for someone with an active lifestyle.

ACTION PLAN
- Go low fat. Aim for 10–15 per cent of your calories on Quickstart, 20–25 per cent when Living Lean.
- Use cold pressed extra virgin olive oil and freshly ground flax seeds as your source of extra fatty acids.
- If you are not vegetarian, eat cold-water fish such as wild trout, wild salmon, mackerel or sardines a couple of times a week or consider supplements of the Omega 3 fatty acids EPA and DHA.
- If you are vegetarian, sprinkle a dessertspoon or tablespoonful of freshly ground vacuum-packed linseeds or flax seeds each day on your cereals or salads or cooked dishes. They have the best balance of linoleic and linolenic essential fatty acids.
- Avoid *all* saturated fats. If you eat meat, only go for the leanest cuts, eat no more than 100 grams at a serving and only once or twice a week, or choose ultra-lean meats like venison or wild boar.
- Avoid highly processed foods. They are riddled with trans fatty acids or junk fats that interfere with your own fatty acid metabolism and impede weight loss.

93

Chapter Seven

Drink Yourself Lean

At the centre of the *Lean Revolution* is *pure* water – lots of
it. Remember that old adage your grandmother used to
chant about drinking 6 to 8 glasses of water a day? Well,
she was right. Except that you may even need *more* than
that. When it comes to shedding excess fat a couple of
extra litres of water a day works wonders.

Water is the most important nutrient of all. It is the stuff
from which your blood, your cells, your muscles – even
your bones – are mostly made. A healthy person who
weights 65 kilos carries about 40 litres of water around –
25 litres inside the cells, 15 litres outside, including 5
litres in the blood. Let yourself become dehydrated and
the chemical reactions in the cells involved in fat burning
become sluggish. Your cells cannot build new tissue efficiently, toxic products build up in your bloodstream,
your blood volume decreases so that you have less oxygen
and nutrients transported to your cells – all of which are
essential to fat burning. Dehydration also results in you
feeling weak and tired and can lead to over-eating as it
disturbs appetite mechanisms so you think you are hungry
even when you are not. The role of water in weight
control and health in general is almost completely
ignored. The brain, too, is 75 per cent water. This is why
the quantity and quality of water you drink also affects

how you think and feel. Thoughts and feelings become distorted when your body gets even mildly dehydrated. For mental clarity and emotional balance you need plenty of water. But if the water you drink is polluted by heavy metals or chemicals then the biochemical reactions on which clear thought and emotional balance depend will become polluted as well.

Liquid Energy

Drinking water liberally brings dynamic energy. When Sir Edmund Hillary set out to conquer Everest he had a shrewd doctor named George Hunt on his ascent team. Hunt knew this precept well. He had studied the records of the recent failed attempt by the Swiss team and discovered that their climbers had drunk less than two glasses of water per day per man. So he ordered special battery-operated snow-melting equipment for the kit and urged the British climbers to take a minimum of twelve glasses of water each day of the climb to reduce their fatigue as they scaled the peaks.

And research with athletes at Harvard University and Loma Linda University in the United States, carried out to explore the relationship between water drinking and energy, has demonstrated that drinking extra water reduces fatigue and stress and increases stamina and energy to a remarkable degree. During one of the Harvard studies, researcher G. C. Pitts set athletes walking at 3½ miles an hour, allowing them to rest regularly, but not allowing them to drink extra water. They reached exhaustion after 3½ hours with temperatures of 102 degrees Fahrenheit. Under the same conditions, he allowed them to drink as much as they wanted. The same athletes lasted 6 hours before collapsing. The third time, the athletes were forced to drink more water than thirst dictated – in quantities calculated by researchers to replace what was being lost in perspiration. This time the athletes were able to continue indefinitely without fatigue or fever until finally, after running out of time, researchers were forced to bring the experiment to a close. Few of us drink as much water as we need to remain in top form. Even if you pay attention to your thirst and quench it regularly you are likely to replace only about a half to two-thirds of the water your body needs for optimal health.

Water Power

Water plays a major part in digesting your food and absorbing nutrients thanks to enzymes which are themselves mostly water. If you fail to drink enough water between meals your mouth becomes low in saliva and digestion suffers. Water is also the medium through which wastes are eliminated from your body. Each time you exhale, you release highly humidified air – about 2 big glasses' worth a day. Your kidneys and intestines eliminate another 6 or so glasses every 24 hours, while another 2 glasses' worth are released through the pores of your skin. That makes 10 glasses a day – and this is on a *cool* day. When it gets hot, when you are exercising, or when you are working hard, the usual 10 glasses lost in this way can triple.

On average, in a temperate climate – not sweating from exertion or heat – we need about 3.5 litres or 6 pints a day for optimal health although few of us consume as much as one third of that. The important thing to remember is that how thirsty you are is *not* a reliable indication of how much water you need to drink. If you want to grow lean and stay that way you need to do as French women have done for decades. Keep a large bottle or two of pure, fresh mineral water within easy reach and make sure you consume your quota of this clear, delicious health-giving drink. Here's how to work it out:

Divide your *current* weight in kilos by 8. If you weigh 58 kilos then 58 divided by 8 equals 7.25 big glasses. Then round the figure upwards to the next glass and there you have it: 8 glasses a day. But remember that is only a base calculation for a cool day. *You will need a lot more during exercise, or on a hot day.*

Provided you do not suffer from a kidney or liver disease, drinking 8 big glasses or more of water a day not only helps you lose weight and keep it off permanently, it improves the functioning of your whole body. This kind of water drinking forms an important part of the total regeneration and weight-loss programmes carried out at the best clinics for natural healing and health education such as Weimar in northern California or the Health Centre for Health Promotion at Loma Linda University.

Hunger Can Be Thirst

The control centre for both thirst and hunger is in the same place in your body: the hypothalamus. Often when you think you are hungry what your body is trying to tell you is that you need to take in more water. Perhaps the best-kept secret in the world about weight control is this: reach for a glass of water every time you feel hungry between meals and you will find your hunger diminishing within a few minutes. Try it and see.

There is another way in which drinking optimal quantities of water plays a central role in fat loss and weight control. It has to do with your kidneys. The kidneys are responsible for recycling all the water in your body – some 800 glasses of it a day – and for filtering out any wastes present before they can lower immunity, create fatigue or make you feel hungry even though you have had enough to eat, and cause the kind of water retention which plagues so many who have gone on and off slimming diets for years. The filtering mechanism responsible for all this in the kidneys is made up of millions of microscopic structures known as *glomeruli*. They identify waste products such as urea which need to be removed as well as screening out other chemicals and unwanted metals and minerals while at the same time pouring back into the bloodstream the minerals you do need and regulating your body's acid-alkaline balance.

When some part of you needs more water, your kidneys make sure it arrives. For instance, when you are hot and sweating a message is sent to the pituitary gland in the head telling it to release the anti-diuretic hormone which in turn tells your kidneys to let more water be resorbed into the blood. Your urine at such times can become highly concentrated and a dark colour. But provided you replenish the water you are losing in sweat by drinking more your kidneys remain happy and well-functioning and the appetite/thirst messages from your brain do not become confused. When your body's water level gets too low, however, your kidneys cannot carry out their cleansing efficiently. Then your liver has to come to the rescue. The trouble is that the liver's main function in weight loss is to mobilize body fat and help transform it into usable energy. When it has to take on some of the kidneys' work the liver is unable to do this effectively. Drinking lots of water – far more than you think you need – helps your kidneys to help your liver to help you lose weight.

Only Water Works

Water is also the world's best natural diuretic. If your body tends to retain water this is often because you don't drink *enough* so it tries its best to hold on to the water there is. Once you do begin to drink *enough* this tendency to waterlogging decreases and usually disappears completely. And, by the way, if you are worried about puckered thighs, the best way to help eliminate them easily is simply to *drink more water*.

What about other drinks – coffee and tea, soft drinks, fruit juices and herb teas? Won't they do just as well? No they won't. Quite apart from the other negative effects of caffeine (an ingredient in coffee, tea and many soft drinks), drinking coffee messes up blood sugar. Caffeine, technically known as trimethyl xanthine, is a habit-form-ing drug. It has frequently been shown to be responsible for headaches, insomnia, nervousness, anxiety, and that familiar wired mental state which keeps you buzzing for a time intellectually but tends to disconnect you from your instincts and in some people even from having a good grip on reality. Caffeine gives you a quick lift and the illusion of energy only to let you crash down a couple of hours later when you are inclined to reach for more – or for a sticky bun or chocolate – just to keep going.

Caffeine has a mutagenic effect too – that is it is capa-ble of crossing the placenta to cause permanent damage to an unborn child as well as breaking apart the chro-mosomes in your own cells and interfering with the repair of DNA. Drinking coffee also stimulates the secretion of acid in your stomach disturbing natural appetite control mechanisms and making you far more likely to end up with an ulcer than your non-coffee-drinking cousin. In fact, caffeine acts as a stimulant to the central nervous system in a rather curious way. It makes you *feel* more mentally alert. But tests show that in reality it creates more confusion and nervousness. In animal experiments very high doses of caffeine have been shown to create psychotic behaviour. Coffee also tends to raise blood pressure and to increase the risk of coronary thrombosis. Drink five cups each day and your heart-attack risk goes up by 60 per cent.

What about tea? It too contains caffeine – 100 mg to coffee's 120 mg in a normal-sized cup. Tea also contains tannic acid – an irritant to the digestive system. In high enough concentrations tannic acid is carcinogenic. There is also evidence that drinking tea in quantity interferes with iron absorption from foods. Even if you have always been a committed 6 to 8 cups a day tea or coffee drinker, after a couple of weeks on good water you will find you don't miss it. Then when you have an occasional cup it becomes a simple pleasure rather than an addiction.

Cut the Soft Drinks

The average intake of soft drinks in the West has risen to 8 to 12 a week in some countries – between 400 and 600 a year. But soft drinks play no part in the *Lean Revolution*. Many colas, squashes and soft drinks also contain caffeine. And they are also far too high in sugar. They bring nutritionally empty calories into your body which you can ill afford. A 330 ml tin of cola contains 7 teaspoons of sugar – about 40 grams. It is full of chemicals to pollute your body and detour your liver's fat elimination processes from its job. Such fizzy drinks are also full of phosphoric acid (the chemical used to etch glass) which, when your body tries to eliminate it via the kidneys, combines with calcium leaching this vital mineral from bones, teeth, nails and hair. Fizzy colas are major contributors to osteoporosis in women.

As for the 'diet' varieties, quite apart from the proven fact that drinking them will do absolutely nothing to help you lose weight, they are an even more chemically polluting cocktail which your body, involved in rebalancing its metabolic processes and shedding excess fat, doesn't need. Fruit juices are okay but remember that they are highly concentrated in sugar. It takes between 3 to 5 oranges to make a glass of juice. So far so good if you drink only 1 glass but when it is hot you probably want to drink even more. If you had to *eat* all those oranges instead you would not eat so many. In hot climates or during the summer months all of us tend to drink too many fruit juices. It is far better to eat the *whole* fruit.

Herb teas such as peppermint, camomile, vervain and lemon grass are also okay. By all means drink them – without sweetening – and enjoy them. But stay away from the fancy packaged ones unless you read the labels carefully and make sure they are entirely natural. Many contain artificial flavours or calories which you don't need. But don't count them into your daily water quota. Think of them as extras. The bottom line is simple: water is best by far. The only problem these days is how do you find water that is fit to drink?

Is Pure Water an Illusion?

The quality of water you drink affects every biochemical reaction on which leanness depends. Hundreds of millions of people in the Western world now drink water contaminated with levels of toxic chemicals far in excess of official standards of safety. Even in sparsely populated countries like Australia, Canada and New Zealand, water is becoming more contaminated each year with toxic heavy metals such as lead, cadmium and aluminium, as well as herbicide and pesticide residues and industrial chemicals – pollutants which are expensive, difficult and sometimes impossible to remove using present water purification methods. In the United States the Environmental Protection Agency, responsible for monitoring the purity of water, have issued official figures that show that as much as 85 per cent of tap water is contaminated to a degree where there is virtually nothing that can be done to improve it significantly. In Britain, by the most conservative estimates, 1.6 million people are now drinking water that breaks the European limits for nitrates alone – quite apart from the 2,000 other possible contaminants. Another 2 million are at risk from high lead and aluminium. As Tom Birch from the environmental pressure group Greenpeace observed as much as five years ago, 'The water authorities and industry are involved in a giant chemistry experiment using the environment as a test tube.'

Impossible Task

What is going on? In theory, our governments are obliged to provide pure water. In practice, however, carrying out this obligation is now so costly that no taxpayer would tolerate the burden. As a result of the ubiquitous environmental pollution worldwide it would be nearly impossible to implement. Nitrates from our farms, acid rain, weed-killers, fertilizers and pesticides, nuclear wastes and the chemical by-products of runaway industrialization have polluted our rivers, dumps, and land-fill sites. From there they seep back into the water table to show up as far as 100 miles away. Even in the most remote regions of Antarctica man-made chemicals such as the polychlorinated bi-phenyls (PCBs) now pollute fish and wildlife despite their living thousands of miles from the so-called civilized world. Yet the public remains largely unaware of how bad it has become.

The technology we still use for cleaning our water is obsolete. We add chlorine, aluminium and other chemicals as part of the attempt to purify water for drinking. Yet many of the chemicals we still use are themselves pollutants that can make matters worse. Chlorine, which we use to kill bacteria, has been linked to the development of anaemia, high blood pressure and diabetes. It reacts with industrial effluent polluting our ground water to form cancer-causing compounds. In the United States, where the awareness of these water problems and water treatment itself is believed to be the most advanced in the world, only 50 of the 60,000 public water systems use up-to-date water purification methods. The whole issue of water pollution and the effect it is having on health – yours and mine – is a huge one far beyond the scope of this little book. But what is important is this: if you want a lean, strong and healthy body you need to find a source of water that is clean.

The Clean-up

This is not an easy task. Most water filters only do part of the job and for any filtering system to work it has to be cleaned and serviced frequently. Boiling your water will kill most bacteria and boil off some of the chlorine but won't move heavy metals and chemical pollutants. Filtering your water through carbon filters will remove pesticides, chlorine and suspended particles but bacteria from contaminated water poured through them tends to colonize and grow between the carbon particles so they need to be cleaned and changed often. Some manufacturers have added silver to these units to inhibit bacterial growth yet silver itself is a contaminant when taken in quantity. This kind of filter won't touch heavy metals like lead and aluminium which have become *dissolved* in the water.

The effective removal of all impurities from water demands large multi-staged and highly complex filter systems operated under carefully controlled conditions. Few home filtering systems are capable of removing anywhere near a cross-section of contaminants. Friends of the Earth will let you have information about how to check out the condition of your own tap water and what your statutory rights are. Put pressure on government and read everything you can on the state of your local and natural water. This is a huge issue for the health of yourself and your family and without massive public pressure is unlikely to change. In the meantime take a good look at what inexpensive jug filters are available and start using one – for cooking too. Be sure to change the filter it contains often and regularly. If you can afford it use the best bottled water for drinking.

Drink Your Health

Bottled waters differ tremendously from one to another. Some which come in plastic containers or glass bottles in the supermarket are nothing more than tap water which has been run through conditioning filters to remove the taste while doing nothing to improve the quality. And just because they say 'spring' on the label that doesn't mean a thing. The word may be nothing more than the brand name used to sell the product. Other bottled waters are excellent in taste and quality. Few countries do much to regulate standards for bottled water and what regulation there is, is generally even poorer than that they apply to tap water. Except in France.

There are some 1,200 springs in France. Several dozen of them supply bottled waters the quality of which has been long monitored and controlled by official government bodies. A few have been granted the title *eau minerale naturelle*. This means that they maintain a constant mineral content. It also means that they have a reputation for specific therapeutic properties. These waters should be safe from bacterial or chemical contamination and you can be sure they have not been mixed with any foreign substance when they are bottled.

Two of the best mineral waters are Volvic, an exceptionally pure still water from the Auvergne mountains in central France, and the sparkling Perrier which arrives in a carbonated form from a spring in Vergèze in southern France. Volvic is lightly mineralized with a lot of character and vibrant quality. The well-known Perrier has long been recommended by French doctors after strenuous exercise. It is a refreshing drink, popular with athletes. I like the taste of it. I also approve of the responsible way in which the Perrier company chose to withdraw hundreds of thousands of bottles from the market a few years ago when they discovered that some had been contaminated with benzene from a faulty filter. It shows a sense of responsibility I would like to see copied by other companies. Finally from the western region of the Vosges mountains in France comes one of the finest of them all: Vittel Bonne Source. Pure and delicate in flavour, Vittel water wends its way through rock tunnels then pours forth clean and fresh from a source surrounded by 12,000 acres of conservation land in north eastern France. Vittel is low in sodium and rich in calcium – an ideal everyday drinking water as part of a Lean Revolution.

Provided you have no kidney disease or other condition which would mean your doctor would disapprove, whatever water you choose to drink, start now to drink a lot of it. So long as your kidneys are normal you need not worry about taking too much. Professor of Paediatrics at Harvard Medical School, Dr Jack Crawford, discovered that healthy adults can tolerate up to 80 glasses of fluid in a day. But drink your water *between* meals not with them. Water drunk with meals dilutes the potency of digestive juices needed to properly break down and assimilate nutrients from your food. It also makes you more likely to over-eat.

Two Each Morning

It takes a bit of practice at first but start by drinking two glasses of water first thing in the morning when you get up either neat or with a twist of lemon or lime. You can heat the water if you like. This helps with elimination. Then drink two or three glasses between breakfast and lunch and another two or three between lunch and dinner. When you exercise or when it is hot remember to drink more. Getting the water habit will quench your appetite, heighten your energy levels, improve the look of your skin and thighs, and help your metabolic processes function at peak. No wonder water power is central to the *Lean Revolution*.

ACTION PLAN

- Cut down on coffee, tea and all soft drinks. As soon as you feel ready cut them out altogether.
- Divide your weight in kilos by eight then round up to the next glass to discover how many 225 ml/8 oz glasses of water to drink each day.
- Drink two glasses of clean water on rising and then get your daily quota by drinking more between meals.
- Keep a bottle or two of mineral water by you during the day as an easy measure of just how much you need to drink to get your daily quota.
- When you are tempted to snack, reach for the water.
- Each trip you make to the toilet (they will become a lot more frequent, although this slows down after the first couple of weeks), give thanks for the deep cleansing which is taking place – as good as a visit to a health spa.
- Sit back and watch your energy increase.

Chapter Eight

Freedom Has Muscle

The next time you have a chance, watch an animal move. Watch the rhythmic lope of a wolf whose body almost becomes the motion; the horse in a field, tossing its mane, pounding its hooves and charging about for sheer pleasure; the dolphin who leaps high in the air twisting its powerful body before disappearing into the waves to emerge a minute later with yet another joyous leap. For many years I wondered why most of us after childhood no longer experience this kind of explosive, rhythmical freedom and energy, grounded in the physical body. Why do we often feel only half alive? And why do those of us who are women tend to look upon our bodies as something separate from ourselves, something to be criticized, judged, or pushed and shoved into shape, instead of celebrating its power and the joy of movement the way animals do. For too many human beings the primary experience of life is one of deadness. And since none of us is able to live with deadness for long we are forced to seek artificial stimulus through drugs or alcohol, compulsive work or sex – just to make us feel alive again. The trouble is, none of the artificial things that we turn to in an attempt to recover our aliveness ever seems to work for very long. Where does the real key lie?

106

Muscle Magic

The answer to this question may surprise you. It stunned me when I first came upon it because it is so simple. The key to aliveness is found in the body itself. It lies in the same place as the key to burning excess fat – in muscle. Your muscle is the engine that turns food calories into energy, burns fat and creates an experience of ongoing simple joy whatever you may be doing. Muscle creates the life-energy for you to think, to move and to feel. The power of the horse, the rhythmical gait of the wolf able to run on and on with ease, the wild playfulness of the dolphin – all depend on good strong muscle. To create a firm, lean body for yourself, begin to listen to, nurture and develop your muscle. The better your muscle the greater your aliveness.

Animal bodies, like ours, are made up of two basic components – *lean body mass* (LBM) which encompasses our muscle tissue and *fat*. Lean body mass – that part which is not fat – is the part of you which is most alive. It consists of your organs such as the heart, the liver, the pancreas, bones and skin, as well as your muscle tissue. Your LBM demands oxygen, uses nutrients from your food, thinks and feels, moves, grows and repairs itself. Wild animals have a high percentage of LBM. That is what gives them their power, their ease of movement, their stamina and their sleek bodies. The rest of you is fat. The hardest thing for most of us to understand who have been brainwashed by low-calorie slimming nonsense is that it is your body's *fat* stores that are the enemy not your weight as measured by the scales.

Fat tissue is very different from your muscle. It does not need oxygen, does not create movement or activity and cannot repair itself. In fact body fat is just about as close as you can get to dead flesh within a living system. Dr Vince Quas, American expert on body change and fat loss and author of an excellent book on the subject, *The Lean Body Promise*, says it better than anyone else I

107

have ever met: 'Your lean body mass *is* you,' he says. 'Your fat is *on* you.'

During a *Lean Revolution* it is the muscle portion of your LBM you will need to work with, both through dietary change and exercise, for it is your LBM that will transform your shape and your energy. It is a fascinating metamorphosis to experience. It does not change you in any intrinsic way, nor does it turn you into someone else's idea of the perfect body. It only makes you more what in essence you really are. What happens is that your lean body mass slowly but inexorably begins to metamorphose a body distorted over the years through stress, poor eating and lack of movement into the true form that is hidden within it.

Body Sculpture

Many years ago I read that Michelangelo claimed never to have sculpted any statues. 'I only took my chisel and removed the extraneous marble in order to reveal the form that was hidden within the stone,' he said. Beginning to be conscious of your own LBM and to work through exercise with that part of it which is muscle sculpts your own body from within. In the process it releases quite astounding levels of energy, creativity and joy. More about the power of LBM in a moment. First let's look more specifically at why exercise – the second element in the *Lean Revolution* – is just as important as a Go Primitive diet.

People sometimes talk about the body as if it were a machine. In reality your body is nothing like a machine. A machine, when you use it, wears out. Your body was designed to be active. The more you use it wisely the stronger and more beautiful it will become, regardless of your age. Lack of exercise or disuse, together with a high-protein diet from excess meat, eggs and dairy products, is the major reason for widespread osteoporosis in women. This weakening of the bones, which is now taking on epidemic proportions in the Western world, develops not as a result of a calcium or oestrogen deficiency as multinational drug companies would have us believe, but rather because we eat a diet far too high in protein which leaches minerals from our systems, and because we have become a culture of couch potatoes. The old adage 'use it or lose it' really applies.

The word is now in: exercise helps prevent degenerative diseases such as cancer and heart disease. An eight-year study which followed more than 10,000 men and 3,000 women and was reported in the *Journal of the American Medical Association* not long ago, looked at the long-term effects of physical fitness. It found that sedentary women (women who are not fit and therefore have a low LBM to fat ratio) were 460 per cent more likely to die early than those that took exercise more regularly. Men in the low fitness category were 340 per cent more likely.

Use It or Lose It

Break your arm and it will shed half its muscle and a third of its bone mass within a few weeks simply because you stop using it. When the cast is taken off it will have shrunk to as little as half its size. If you are forced for any reason to stay in bed for a few months the loss of minerals from your bones and the ageing of your muscle tissue can speed up by ten years. That is the bad news. Here is the good news: your body responds amazingly to exercise – even to a little of it. Not only will your muscles grow stronger and smoother, but your bone tissue will become denser. Stop exercising again and your body turns to flab, your energy levels drop, your muscle mass shrinks (as does your ability to burn calories), and with it goes your overall sense of wellbeing.

What kind of exercise do you need for permanent weight control? Not the kind that goes all out to burn as many calories as possible. Far from it. That only *depletes* your energy, *slows* fat burning and leaves you feeling exhausted and looking haggard. Exercise for fat loss needs to be slow, sustained and regular and it needs to do three things: enhance your metabolism, increase your supply of oxygen to the mitochondria of muscle cells for fat burning and shift the ratio of your body's LBM to fat in favour of muscle. For this you need two kinds of exercise – *aerobic*, such as brisk walking, to stimulate oxygen supply, and *muscle-enhancing*, such as weight training or the Royal Canadian Air Force XBX Plan.

Fat is Dead

Because your body's fat tissues have a very low metabolic activity, they don't burn calories. Only mitochondria in your muscle cells do this. The more muscle tissue you have the better your body burns calories, sheds fat and keeps it off. Also the more muscle you have the more you are able to eat without gaining weight. But you need a lot of oxygen to do this. In fact the more oxygen your muscles are supplied with via the bloodstream the more calories and fat your body can burn. When we eat a high-fat diet as we do in the West the rate at which your blood transports oxygen to the cells is greatly slowed down. Fat in the blood makes red blood cells – the oxygen carriers – clump together. This happens very quickly after eating a meal rich in fat.

Aerobic exercise enhances your body's oxygen transport and use. It could be running, walking, swimming, cycling or any other activity which uses the large muscle groups and where your heart beats steadily and you breathe deeply for a period of 20–45 minutes at least three, preferably four, times a week. Aerobic exercise enhances overall fitness and wellbeing in other ways too. It improves the functioning of the heart, lowers cholesterol, and shifts brain chemistry so that you produce natural opiates which make you feel good. It also increases noradrenaline – a brain chemical which improves your self-image and confidence so you feel better about yourself and your life all round. Noradrenaline and its sister hormone adrenaline (which also increases with regular exercise) both stimulate the fat-burning ability of the mitochondria. Aerobic exercise enhances fat burning not only while you are working out but for many hours afterwards as well. Interesting weight-loss studies show that in many cases aerobic exercise alone can bring about weight loss. Shedding weight while exercising regularly means that you lose fat instead of water or vital lean tissue. Once you get into it you'll come to love it, while I have never met anyone who enjoys dieting!

To make use of aerobic exercise as part of your *Lean Revolution* it must *not* be high-intensity. When you exercise too hard or become breathless while working out the energy which feeds your movement is drawn not from your fat stores but from glycogen in your liver and your muscles. Exercise that works best is *moderate*, aerobic and of *long* duration since this kind burns both glycogen *and* fat. After 30 minutes of brisk sustained walking your body makes an important shift so that only 50 per cent of its energy comes from glycogen and the rest from your fat stores. Studies in exercise physiology suggest that the minimal threshold of exercise training to shed fat demands continuous movement of at least 20–30 minutes, duration and at least three times a week. Less than that and you are really wasting your time. The important thing to remember about fat burning is to exercise not *hard* but *long*.

Watch Your Heart

Most exercise physiologists who work with weight control suggest that you walk, or carry out whatever other activity you have chosen, at 70–85 per cent of your maximum heart rate (MHR), but some recent studies suggest that exercising at as little as 45 per cent of MHR will do the trick nicely. To get your maximum heart rate, subtract your age from 220. So if you are 36 years old your MHR would be $220 - 36 = 184$. From this figure you can calculate your ideal aerobic range by multiplying that number by 0.45 for the low end and 0.85 for the high. Aim for somewhere in the middle unless you are very unfit in which case go for the lower figure.

Here's how to take your pulse. After a few minutes of exercising stop and put three fingers over your radial artery – on the thumb side of your wrist – to find your heart beat. Using a watch with a second hand count the number of heart beats over a period of 15 seconds then multiply this by 4 and you will know immediately if you are working out in the right range. As part of your *Lean Revolution* you need to create for yourself a minimum exercise programme. Choose one of the following:

- walking 30–45 minutes three times a week (best of all for most people).
- cycling 40–45 minutes 3–5 times a week.
- jogging, 30–45 minutes 3–5 times a week.
- rowing, 30–45 minutes, 3–5 times a week.
- swimming, 30–45 minutes, 3–5 times a week.

So-called aerobics classes are not a true form of aerobics exercise. Some of them are far too hard so that you burn glycogen instead of fat and others are start/stop so that you don't get a consistent aerobic effect.

Muscle and Transformation

Now let's go back to lean body mass (LBM) for there lies the second exercise secret to permanent weight control. Your LBM is always changing – increasing or decreasing. When it changes this is not because of alterations in your organs or bones but rather because of alterations in your muscle. Under-muscled people have low levels of energy. Studies show they are at as great a risk from degeneration and early ageing as people who are over-fat. When your muscles are strong and dense and alive, aches and pains vanish. When muscles are in tone your posture is good too for posture depends upon muscle alone. So does the proper elimination of waste from your cells. The lymphatic system which carries waste products away is not powered by the heart but by muscle movement. The more muscle movement you get the better it works. This is particularly important for women – even slim women. For unless your lymphatic system is working properly you can end up with deposits of water, wastes and fat on localized areas of your body, better known as cellulite. To shed fat and keep it off you need to increase your LBM. For energy, beauty, health and weight control, most physiologists would say that 90 per cent LBM to only 10 per cent fat is ideal for men. For women, 80–85 per cent LBM is just about perfect, which means carrying no more than 15–20 per cent of your weight in fat.

How your body performs biochemically as well as physiologically is determined by the ratio of LBM to fat. When for any reason, such as being inactive or going off and on slimming diets, you shed lean muscle tissue, your energy and the way your body performs is undermined. In most of us this is a slow decrease, often so slow that you don't notice it, only to awaken in mid-life to find that your body is flabby even if you have remained thin and that you suffer from chronic fatigue. There are other things, too, that can decrease muscle mass such as illness or too much exercise, or the wrong kind of exercise. Then, even if you appear to have stayed the same weight on the scales, the fat on your body will have increased and your body will have lost a great deal of its tone. The important thing to remember about weight control is this: stop worrying about how to whittle away just a bit more flab from your hips, thighs or tummy and concentrate instead on improving your muscle mass.

Check it Out

There are a number of methods for measuring body composition. They are most often used by physiologists concerned with improving the performance of athletes.

113

It is sometimes done in sports clinics by hydrostatic weighing – that is immersing your body in a large tub of water and then weighing you when you are entirely under water. For your LBM is heavy and the fat on your body is lighter than water, which is why fat people tend to float very easily when they swim. Sometimes physiologists use what is called an impedance unit where a very small current is sent through pads placed on your wrists or ankles to determine LBM-to-fat ratios; or sound or light waves are sent through the body. These methods, too, can give quite an accurate reading of the fat/lean body mass measurement because your muscle tissue is heavier in water, which is a better conductor of electricity than is fat, so the current travels faster when you have a lot of muscle tissue.

The most common way of measuring – although not by any means the most accurate – is with skin callipers where you pinch your skin at various parts of the body then measure the thickness of the pinch and do some complex calculations to determine LBM-to-fat ratio. This method is a lot less accurate than the others but is a lot easier to carry out! Easiest of all is to reach down and pinch your own flesh with your fingers at the area at the bottom of the ribs, on your thighs, upper arms, belly, bottom and hips. If your pinch is thicker than 1–2.5 cm (half an inch to one inch), your LBM-to-fat ratio is not as good as it could be.

Forget Your Age

There is a widespread belief that as you get older your body metabolism naturally slows down and therefore you are less and less able to prevent yourself from becoming fat. Actually, age has absolutely nothing to do with it. It doesn't matter how old you are or how much you weigh now. What limits your ability to burn fat and stay lean is how long you have been inactive. It is long-term inactivity that wastes LBM and results in the mitochondria being unable to burn the calories you take in from wholesome food as energy. Start now to improve your LBM by increasing the amount of muscle in your body and you can forget the days of calorie counting for ever. Once your LBM becomes prominent enough you will become one of those people you have always envied, who can eat whatever they like without ever gaining weight. But you have got to exercise to keep it that way.

That is where exercise designed specifically for building muscle comes in. Don't worry, this does not mean that you will end up with a killer body like Madonna. Quite the contrary. Exercise to build muscle, such as weight training using very light weights but many repetitions, is the most effective way of building LBM and uncovering your true body form. It chisels and defines arms, legs, torso, hips and bottom, even if they have been neglected for many years and have lost their natural tone and shape. So good is this kind of body building at improving LBM that until recently no one considered that it might be an excellent form of protecting against degenerative diseases such as coronary heart disease as well. There was a time when aerobic exercise was considered king for health, fitness and longevity. Now, thanks to new research into the effects of weight training at prestigious centres such as McMasters University in Ontario, we know that aerobic exercise combined with weight training is the very best you can get for health, fitness and longevity as well as stamina and energy. As a result, the much-respected American College of Sports Medicine has recently revised its long-standing assertion that aerobic exercise held the key. Its new programme advises a minimum of two sessions of weight training a week using ten different exercises to enhance the large muscles of the chest, back and legs as well as three sessions of aerobic exercise. When it comes to bringing about your *Lean Revolution* you can't do better than that.

Many sports centres throughout the world now offer excellent weight-training equipment and instructors to teach you how to use it at very little cost. Even if you have never tried any form of weight training before you might enrol at one and have a go. If, for any reason you are housebound, get yourself a copy of the Royal Canadian Air Force *XBX Plan*. There is one for men and one for women. These are free-standing exercises with similar effects which you can do at home. They take only about 12 minutes to carry out, four days a week, and can be done virtually anywhere. In three months' time you will not only be delighted with the way your body is changing form and redefining itself, you are likely to feel better about yourself than you have ever done in your life. Such are the rewards of *Lean Revolution* exercise.

ACTION PLAN

- Start today to exercise – walking is good. If you are not used to exercise begin with only 10 minutes a day and work up gradually adding another 10 minutes every few days.
- Find a friend and make a pact to exercise together 4 or 5 times a week, join a gym or get support from family and friends.
- Experiment with different kinds of exercise to find out which you enjoy most. Enjoyment is an important factor in making exercise work for you.
- Make a note of how you feel on the days you do and don't exercise and compare them.
- Let yourself daydream about how your body will change in the next few months. The imagination is a potent tool to drive your *Lean Revolution*.

Chapter Nine

Lean Manifesto

Lean Revolution is not some stringent programme you put yourself on, hold your breath and hope for the best. Far from it. It is a slow and gradual transformation of your lifestyle – the foods you eat, the way that you exercise, the attitude that you take towards your body. With Go Primitive what you will be instigating is a total life change, of remarkable breadth with almost unlimited potential for self-transformation. That is not the kind of thing anyone should jump into carelessly.

If a Go Primitive way of eating is brand new to you, the best way to get into it is through small, progressive changes, day by day and week by week. If you are a big meat eater begin by reducing the amount of meat that you eat and choose only the leanest types of meat taken twice a week instead of every day. Then cut down to perhaps once a week or once every two weeks until you find that it is quite natural to let the amount of meat that you eat dwindle to practically nothing. You can do the same with fish and milk products – cheese, eggs and other high-fat dairy foods, sweets and alcohol.

Meanwhile give yourself a chance to experiment with some of the recipes in Chapter 10. You will discover that far from being in any way a diet of deprivation, both the Quickstart and the Living Lean phases of Go Primitive are full of exciting dishes that make use of a great variety of foods, flavours and textures. Begin by trying one or two of them for your main meal and start to eat a good breakfast every day based on the breakfast recipes. You will be surprised to find that almost all the dishes that you cook for yourself will be loved by others you may have to cook for, even if their interpretation of them includes a topping of butter, whipped cream or the odd Scotch egg.

New Elite

Go Primitive eating is not the province of slimmers. It forms the basis of the very best nutrition that you can find for athletes, children, men concerned about preventing coronary heart disease – even for entertaining. There was a time when beans and pulses were looked down on. Nowadays, amongst the new elite groups – athletes, models, people in the public eye – they form the basis of a way of eating that keeps you young, vibrant and able to rise at 5 a.m. if necessary, and work long hours on a film set without losing your cool or undermining your good looks. Where, even ten years ago, all the food talk was of smoked salmon paté, now you are more likely to come across some stunningly beautiful model, or audacious athlete preparing for the Iron Man triathlon in Hawaii, expounding on the virtue of a new recipe they have just discovered for vegetarian chilli. Most fashions are frivolous and carry little weight when it comes to influencing your life. Go Primitive – which is rapidly becoming the food style of the highly motivated and the physically elite – is different. It has the power not only to intrigue but to transform one's body and one's life at the deepest levels.

The vegetables and dried beans and grains which are the backbone of this kind of eating have superb colours and textures. They vary so much from one to another and there are so many intriguing ways of preparing them that one could go on creating meals made from them for several weeks without ever having to repeat the same dish – lasagne, hearty stews, cream soups, spiky salads with intriguing sauces, braised fruit pies – all well within the 15 per cent fat level of Quickstart. Experiment with them but remember to introduce them slowly into whatever diet you have been used to. This is for two reasons. First, changing your diet dramatically in any direction can cause digestive upset simply because the human body tends to rebel against whatever it is not accustomed to. This is particularly important when introducing beans, peas and lentils into your life. The balance of intestinal flora – the micro-organisms which produce many of the B-complex vitamins in your body – varies tremendously with the kind of foods you are used to. Give yourself a chance. Let them re-balance a bit before bombarding yourself with piles of beans. The second and more important reason to ease into Go Primitive is that the changes that are made slowly are the changes that *last*. Begin by making one meal a day on Go Primitive principles and notice how much better you feel in a week or two. You will quite naturally be encouraged to increase your intake of these wonderfully varied low-fat foods. This way the process of change becomes a natural evolution from your old diet to your new.

Big Breakfast

Try beginning each day with a good breakfast and cutting down on the amount you eat in the evening. The two very much go together, for after a light evening meal you will find that your own natural hunger in the morning will begin to show itself. Meanwhile, enjoy your steak if you want it or your cream bun. I would never do anything to restrain myself from eating a piece of chocolate cake if I felt I wanted it. It is just that having tried enough pieces of chocolate cake and knowing what it feels like to eat such foods, you find that after a while you don't want them any more. Fresh strawberries, drizzled in mango topping, become infinitely more appealing.

As far as alcohol is concerned, it is not excluded from a Go Primitive diet. But neither is it encouraged. Highly concentrated and quickly absorbed, alcohol is not only easily transformed into fat within your body, it also tends to disturb the blood-sugar curve and unsettle the appetite. Have a drink and false appetite often appears within urging you to eat more than your body really wants. Also, alcohol is toxic to a number of the organs in the body, particularly the liver, and finally, like sugar, alcohol provides a lot of extra calories but no nutrition. By all means do enjoy the occasional glass of wine. But you may find, as most who Go Primitive do, that your body soon becomes highly sensitive to alcohol and drugs and that you feel so well you no longer want that drink in the evening to undermine your energy even if you have long been accustomed to taking it.

Forget Deprivation – Enjoy

What is important always to remember is that Go Primitive is in no way a diet of deprivation. It is, on the contrary, a pathway to freedom – a road you will walk in your own way, adapting its basic principles to your own work patterns, food preferences and lifestyle. Although you never need to count calories on Go Primitive, you will want to read labels carefully on any commercially prepared products to make sure that they fall well within the fat range of 10–15 per cent during the Quickstart phase and 20–25 per cent during Living Lean. It is also a very good idea to keep a checklist day by day for the simple purpose of making you aware of the rate at which you are making dietary and lifestyle changes as part of your own *Lean Revolution*. Here is one that I have adapted from a Weimar Institute chart given to me by Vincent Gardner MD. I find it particularly useful since a major factor while shedding excess weight is being conscious of one's actions – particularly if you lead a very busy and active life. The chart lasts for a week. It can be photo-

GO PRIMITIVE CHECKLIST

Day	1		2		3		4		5		6		7	
ACTIVITY	Yes	No	Yes	No	Yes	No	Yes	No	Yes	No	Yes	No	Yes	No
Ate light or no supper														
Ate good breakfast														
Ate no snacks														
Drank adequate water														
Took no caffeine														
Drank little or no alcohol														
Ate only at meal times														
No other activity while eating														
Ate slowly														
Used a wide variety of foods														
Ate no convenience foods														
Kept refined foods at a minimum														
Kept free-fats at a minimum														
Exercised adequately														
Got enough rest														
Handled stress effectively														
Made time for contemplation or relaxation														

Note: Adapted from the Weimar Institute Chart used by Vincent Gardner MD.

copied a number of times and used over and over again for as long as you want. I would suggest at least the first 6 to 8 weeks of Go Primitive and then periodically for 2- or 3-week periods as you progress. It is always useful to go back to. It is also helpful if you are travelling or have been living through a stressful period where you have been rather careless about what you have been eating. It helps re-orientate the direction of your own *Lean Revolution* so that you are clear not only about where you are going but how rapidly you are getting there.

One very important aspect of the *Lean Revolution is* variety. Archaeological studies of the mummified remains of our ancestors show that 10,000 years ago they consumed over 200 different varieties of plant foods. We in the West consume a couple of dozen. The greater the variety of plant foods that you eat the more diverse is the supply of various minerals, vitamins, trace elements and other micro-nutrients that you take in. This is an important consideration in meal planning as is making sure you get plenty of green vegetables each day.

Like a King

Go Primitive is based around two large meals a day: breakfast which should supply between a third and a half of all the calories for the day, and a main meal – best eaten at lunchtime or at least before 4 o'clock in the afternoon if you can possibly manage it – with a very light meal of salad or fruit with some toast in the evening. Later on you will probably want no evening meal at all. In between meals it is important to drink your quota of water. Begin with 2 large glasses in the morning just as soon as you get up, and then again throughout the morning, afternoon and evening until all you intended to drink is finished. The one time when you don't drink water on Go Primitive is at meal times since water can dilute the digestive systems and interfere with the efficiency of digestion and absorption. It is important to reach for a glass or even two of water whenever you happen to feel hungry between meals. It is absolutely the best appetite suppressant in the world and every time you drink a glass you are cleansing your body as well as quenching any false appetite that may arise from stress.

Here are some general guidelines that you may find useful to refer to.

GUIDELINES FOR GO PRIMITIVE

- Eat a big breakfast, a good main meal in the middle of the day and the lightest of suppers, or no supper at all, preferably 2 to 3 hours or even more before going to bed.
- Avoid eating between meals since this slows the stomach from emptying and encourages food still in the stomach to ferment as well as creating false appetite.
- Leave 5 hours between meals – the time your body needs to efficiently and completely digest the previous meal.
- Make meal times a pleasure. Eat slowly and chew your foods thoroughly. Not only will this increase your enjoyment of the food, it will also mean that you digest your foods properly, that you don't end up with digestive disturbances including gastric wind, and that you don't over-eat.
- Drink lots of water – enough to make your urine quite pale – but always *between* meals. Give yourself 20 minutes water-free before a meal and half an hour afterwards.
- Vary your foods from meal to meal so that you get a great variety over a period of a month, but don't eat too many different foods at one meal as this can challenge the digestive system.
- As much as you can, choose foods that are grown on healthy soils and eaten in their wholeness as closely as possible to the way they come from nature.

123

You are likely to find, as I have, that within two weeks of beginning Go Primitive any false appetite disappears so that very seldom do you need to reach for a snack even when you are aware that your body doesn't really need the food. This was one of the things that it most surprised me to discover. I have always been most hungry in the evenings. I was someone who could often go all day long without eating only to find that when the sun went down I could think of nothing but food. With Go Primitive eating I soon found that not only did my night hunger disappear, I soon began to thoroughly enjoy a large breakfast and lunch and then to actually look forward to the evenings and the nights when I didn't have to eat. It has given me more time to do the things I want to do and I have come to delight in the lightness of the experience and in the rest that my body gets at night – every bit as much as I enjoy my meals. I also love the way that I feel from not eating all the foods heavy in fat that I used to eat. I get much pleasure from my increased energy, I need less sleep, I feel calmer. Meanwhile the excess fat on my body slowly and steadily decreases without my ever worrying about it. I also find that I can think more clearly than I could before.

The reason that so many of our foods are high in fat and the reason that so many fats are put into convenience foods is that fat tastes good. Fat was always my favourite food. It takes a little time to get used to low-fat eating, so be patient. What you will find surprising is that after several weeks of Go Primitive eating you begin to lose your taste for fat so that when someone offers you a dish covered with cream sauce you will actually find it rather unpleasant. I would never have believed this to be true. Most of my life I could have sat down and eaten a whole avocado for lunch without blinking. Now I enjoy what fats there are in my food but am really quite put off by any food served me which has cream or butter in it or too much olive oil. So much of food preference is based on habit. Be patient and new habits will replace old quite naturally.

It is a similar situation with salt. You will notice that few of the Go Primitive recipes call for salt and those that do use only the tiniest bit – a pinch, no more. Putting salt on food is more of a ritual than anything else. As you decrease the amount of salt you eat, relying instead on some of the wonderful herbs and seasonings available, you will find that you begin to taste your foods better than you did before and that you are more aware of the wonderful textures and distinctive flavours. Within two weeks to a month you are likely to have lost the craving for all that salt you once ate. There is plenty of salt in foods themselves without adding more. Eating too much salt contributes to hardening of the arteries, high blood pressure in those who are prone to it, and disturbs the natural sodium/potassium balance in the body, making you retain water.

Be Creative

The recipes in the next chapter are only suggestions. I hope that you will use them as inspiration to create your own recipes. It is also quite easy to adapt your favourite recipes to a *Lean Revolution* lifestyle by taking out the oils and fats they call for and substituting other ingredients. Take a look at the Go Primitive recipes and you will soon get the knack. When planning your menus the principles are simple. Eat breakfast like a king, eat lunch like a prince and supper like a pauper. And by all means have a cup of herb tea or coffee substitute with your breakfast if you would usually have a warm drink. On the next page are the general principles of Go Primitive eating followed by a sample meal planner for a fortnight to give you an idea of how it all works.

Glycosport or Glycoslim (see Chapter 5) can be of great help particularly in the Quickstart phase of Go Primitive, and most especially right at the beginning to carry you through the transition period and help you overcome any blood-sugar or energy problems you may have inherited from the way you ate before. Glycosport

BREAKFAST	MAIN MEAL	LIGHT MEAL (or no meal at all)
A grain dish, i.e. porridge, raw muesli, crêpes, granola. One or two pieces of fruit. Whole-grain bread, muffin or toast and a fruit or nut spread.	A main course plus some raw vegetables – crudités, salads or sprouted seeds and grains, plus a yellow and a green vegetable if not already incorporated. Whole-grain bread with a fruit or protein spread.	A fruit dish, or fresh fruit salad, or a light soup.

and Glycoslim are virtually the same. The original product – Glycosport – was made for athletes and people with active lifestyles. Glycoslim is a version of the product designed for people losing weight. Buy whichever is least expensive. Mix it with a very small quantity of fruit juice or one of the fruit drinks such as Sao Rico or Aqualibra and take between meals. It will not disturb your stomach's 'rest' periods.

Eating Out

Eating out is not as great a challenge as you might imagine. I travel a great deal and I have been able to find foods that fit nicely into both the Quickstart and the Living Lean phases of Go Primitive in every city I have been in. If the worse comes to the worst you can even plunder a salad bar in a fast-food restaurant provided you choose the bits and pieces carefully. The better restaurants make life a great deal easier. These days restaurant managers are not at all taken aback by someone making special dietary requests. When it is feasible call ahead and speak to the chef or manager, explaining that you do not eat any free-fats and asking what in particular they would suggest from their menu.

	WEEK ONE	
	BREAKFAST	**MAIN MEAL**
Monday	Munchy-Crunchy Granola with soya milk or skimmed milk Rye toast with fruit spread A fresh peach Breakfast drink	Easy Vegetable Curry Sprout Salad with Balsamic Dressing Melon
Tuesday	Raisin & Cinnamon Oat Porridge with soya or skimmed milk topped with grated apple Half a grapefruit & a tangerine Breakfast drink	Crudité with Mock Guacamole Pizza Fresh fruit salad
Wednesday	Raisin Bran Muffins spread with Apple Butter Fresh fruit salad Breakfast drink	Curried Pumpkin Soup Ginger Sweet Potatoes Jungle Slaw Orange Sorbet
Thursday	Raw Apple Muesli Whole-grain wheat toast Fresh strawberries & mango Breakfast drink	Oat Burgers High-fibre Salad Baked Carrots Lemon Pie
Friday	Corn Meal with fruit topping Sliced oranges & plumped raisins Breakfast drink	Baby Lima Bean Salad Pumpkin in Tahini Baked Apples
Saturday	Cracked Wheat Cereal with Date Butter Sliced peaches Raisin toast Breakfast drink	Luscious Lentil Soup Brown Rice Salad Prune Whip
Sunday	Scrambled tofu with oven-fried chips & garlic bread Half a cantaloup melon stuffed with blueberries Breakfast drink	Barley Pilaff with Miso Sauce Minty Peas Winter Chunk Salad Raspberry Sorbet

WEEK TWO		
	BREAKFAST	**MAIN MEAL**
Monday	Raisin & Cinnamon Oat Porridge with soya or skimmed milk Fresh orange juice Toast with fruit spread Breakfast drink	Dahl Stew Yummy Brown Rice Crisp Carrot Salad Alfalfa sprouts Stuffed Pineapple
Tuesday	Apple Bread Pudding with apricot topping Half a grapefruit Mixed grain toast spread with strawberry jam Breakfast drink	Split Pea Soup Tossed green salad with croûtons Jacket Potatoes with Tofu Dip
Wednesday	Best Breakfast Crêpes drizzled with pear topping Nectarines & sliced oranges Breakfast drink	Chilli with Corn Bread Apple Ginger Salad with added watercress
Thursday	Munchy-Crunchy Granola with soya or skimmed milk topped with sliced banana Tangerines & green grapes Breakfast drink	Thick Vegetable Soup Kasha with Toasted Sesame Topping Fresh watercress with Tomato Vinaigrette Banana Cream Pie
Friday	Baked Breakfast Pudding Sliced pineapple & oranges Breakfast drink	Curried Pumpkin Soup Artichokes Fresh herb & flower salad with Sprout Salad Dressing Whole-grain rolls spread with Aubergine Paté
Saturday	Banana muesli Fresh strawberries Rye toast & blueberry jam Breakfast drink	Vegetable Stew Sprout Salad with Ginger Dressing Rice Cakes Pineapple Blackberry Frappé

WEEK TWO (Continued)	
BREAKFAST	**MAIN MEAL**
Sunday Feather Light Waffles with raspberry topping Half a grapefruit & fresh berries Orange juice Breakfast drink	Black-eyed Peas with thick rye bread spread with Raw Hummus Italian Salad

Boiling, steaming and baking do not demand the addition of any oil. Steer clear of foods that are fried, creamed, au gratin, or sautéed. Ask if they will prepare something for you without butter or oil, and always request that any sauces come as side dishes – not poured over the food that you have ordered. Almost every decent restaurant these days has fresh fruit for dessert, or even a fruit sorbet. Many restaurants have vegetarian main dishes but get them to leave off the greasy cheese or sour cream. If you find one that doesn't have vegetarian dishes, and you don't want to eat fish or meat, order a soup or a salad as a first course and a plate of steamed or wok-fried vegetables, or two or three starters to follow. If you fancy a chef's salad, simply ask them to leave the meat and cheese off it and request that they use lemon juice or vinegar, garlic and pepper, instead of oil as salad dressing. You can also order a plate of vegetables and ask that the chef does not use any oil or butter in their preparation. The best Chinese restaurants are great for Go Primitive. Some even use dry-wok cooking, a technique for sautée-ing vegetables without oil. This, together with steamed rice, is fine, even if the rice happens to be white, but stay away from fried rice which is cooked in oils. When you are invited out to dinner at someone's house, explain to your hosts beforehand that you do not eat oils or butter and, if necessary, have something to eat before you go so you are not too hungry.

One of the great pleasures of food in our culture is

eating out with friends and this very often takes place in the evening. I learned a useful trick in handling this situation from Dr Vincent Gardner, Coordinator of the Professional Observer Programme at the Weimar Institute. If you are out in the evening and eat a meal that is heavier than you would like you can easily make up for it the next day by having a good hearty breakfast then skipping both lunch and supper. You might want to increase your water intake that day, too, as a means of deep cleansing your body. This way you can enjoy an evening with friends yet very quickly get back into the Go Primitive rhythm without pangs of guilt and disappointment or feeling that you have undermined your own *Lean Revolution*.

Slow and Steady Does It

The most important thing to remember is that the lifestyle changes which you are instigating with Go Primitive and by making a place for exercise in your life, do not belong to some rigid programme where you have to grit your teeth and bear it. Far from it. They are the means by which, given time, you can discover your own pathway to freedom. This pathway will only be found slowly and steadily over time as you discover what works best in your own life and make readjustments to suit you. There will be moments when the general principles set out in Go Primitive seem to be forgotten. These times are of no great significance. If one morning you sit down and eat half a pound of chocolate, it is no big deal. Indeed, by being aware of how it makes you feel both then and afterwards, such an experience can empower you even further in your commitment to your own freedom. For it is you who are in control and it is you who make the choices about your own life. This is the major learning experience for each one of us as we walk our own path on the *Lean Revolution*. The freedom that comes with discovering this is of an order which cannot be described. It is something you must discover for yourself.

Chapter Ten

Go Primitive

Go Primitive foods are special and so is buying them. You will find your larder stocked with a whole new set of ingredients – particularly if, until now, you have been living on convenience foods or meat and two veg. The foods which you will use for most of these recipes are not only good for you, they are delicious – grains and legumes, nuts and seeds, fruits, vegetables and herbs.

These foods can either be bought at great cost or, if you shop around, very cheaply. Because I have a large family I buy many of my fruits in crates from a wholesaler at less than half the price I would pay at the greengrocer. You can pay dearly for nuts, seeds, grains and pulses in some health-food stores where they come in tiny packages (and are often not very fresh). But beans and legumes, nuts and seeds can also be bought cheaply in good super-markets or in bulk at reasonable cost from many of the new whole-food emporiums which are beginning to appear everywhere. Obviously the more you buy at one time the cheaper they are. Be sure to refrigerate your nuts after purchase to keep their oils from going rancid. And if ever you buy a package of anything which you find on returning home is not absolutely fresh, take it back and complain. That is the only way to protect your-self while improving the quality of what is being sold.

Here is a brief guide to stocking a *Lean Revolution* larder to give you some idea of just how much variety you have to choose from.

FRUIT

Not only are fruits some of the most delicious natural foods available, they also have remarkable properties for spring-cleaning the body and are excellent biochemical antidotes to stress. Because fruits contain many natural acids such as citric and malic acid, they have an acid pH reaction in digestion. However, since they are also a rich source of alkaline-forming minerals, their reaction in the blood is always alkaline. This reaction helps neutralize the acid by-products of stress as well as the waste products of metabolism which are also acidic. That is why fruits are so highly prized as a means of internally cleansing the body.

Fruit contains very little protein but it is very high in the mineral potassium which needs to be balanced with sodium for perfect health in the body. Because most people in the West eat far too much sodium in the form of table salt and an excess of protein as well (which leaches important minerals from the bones and tissues), eating good quantities of fruit can help re-balance a body, improve its functioning, and make you feel more energetic as well.

Finally, because fruits are naturally sweet and because we are born with an innate liking for sweet things, a dessert of fresh fruit after a meal can be tremendously satisfying to the palate. And there is such a variety of beautiful textures, colours and tastes to choose from – from the sensuous softness of persimmons and the super-sweetness of fresh figs, to the exhilarating crunch of the finest English apple.

VEGETABLES

The best vegetables are those you grow yourself organically. If you are lucky enough to have a garden – even a small one – save all the leftovers and turn them into compost for fertilizer. Even in winter you can grow some delicious salads and root vegetables in a greenhouse or under cloches. The quality of organic produce is far superior to chemically fertilized fruits and vegetables – not to mention all the vitamins which are lost in foods when they are picked, stored, shipped and sit on shop shelves. In summer I go to the garden to pick my vegetables and fifteen minutes later they are gracing the dinner table. And if you are a flat dweller without a garden there is nothing to stop you from sprouting fresh seeds and grains in jars or trays on your windowsill (see page 140).

How you treat your vegetables once you cut them or buy them from the shops determines a lot how they taste and how much of their energy-enhancing goodness you preserve. Scrub anything that will stand up to a good scrubbing, using a brush marked *veg only*. Scrubbing vegetables is better than peeling since many of the valuable vitamins and minerals are stored directly beneath their skins. Never soak vegetables for long periods. They are better washed briefly under running water so you don't allow water-soluble vitamins to leach out of them. Always keep vegetables as cool as possible (even carrots and turnips are best kept in the fridge) and use them as soon as you can. When shopping for fresh things be demanding – choose your own cauliflower and make sure it is a good one. Don't be intimidated by pushy greengrocers who want to foist the leftovers on you before they bring in their new stock. Demand the best and you will get it. Your palate and your health will be grateful that you do.

GRAINS

Thousands of years ago Zarathustra, the Persian sage, waxed ecstatic about grains. 'When the light of the moon waxeth warmer,' he said, 'golden hued grains grow up from the earth during the spring.' I have always thought his words beautifully captured the richness and delight of the grain foods, the most important single foods in Go Primitive. When a good portion of what you eat comes from grain foods – because of the effect on the brain of the complex carbohydrates they contain – it tends to improve one's disposition, making you feel calm and bringing you energy that lasts and lasts. Grains, like legumes, need special handling. They should not be eaten raw. This is why many of the packaged mueslis cause digestive upset in many people. It is only by cooking them (or by sprouting or soaking them) that you turn hard-to-digest starches into more easily digested sugars. All grains can be toasted lightly. This process, which is called dextrinizing, not only helps turn starches into natural sugars but also enhances the flavour of grains used as cereals or cooked in other recipes.

To dextrinize grains, spread them on a baking sheet and pop them into an oven at 150°C (300°F) Gas 2 for about 20 minutes, stirring every now and then. This is not necessary if you are going to boil them, but it does enhance the flavour and is particularly good if you want to use grains to make porridge or other hot breakfast cereals. The other important thing to remember about grains is that it is best to get as wide a variety as possible so if you have oat porridge at breakfast, at lunch you might choose whole rye bread or a bulgur wheat salad or brown rice. The more variety the better since each grain boasts a different balance of essential minerals and micro-nutrients.

OILS

Go Primitive does not use oils, except a very small quantity of cold-pressed soya oil or extra virgin olive oil. In heat-processed oils usable 'cis' fatty acids have been chemically changed into 'trans' fatty acids – junk fats – which can not only be actively harmful, but actually block the use of any 'cis' fatty acids in the rest of your diet. Olive oil adds a distinctive flavour to salad dressings. It is quite heavy though and some people prefer a lighter oil. Sesame is lighter and delicious too. Cold-pressed walnut oil, if you can get it, is delicious for salads and full of essential fatty acids but it is expensive and must be kept in the fridge.

134

GUIDE TO COOKING GO PRIMITIVE GRAINS

Grain (1 cup)	Water (cups)	Cooking time	Yield (cups)
Barley (whole)	4–5	2–3 hours	3½
Barley (flakes)	3	45–60 minutes	3
Brown rice	2–2½	1 hour	3
Buckwheat	2	20 minutes	2½
Bulgur wheat	2	15–20 minutes	2½
Couscous	1	15 minutes	2¾
Millet	2½–3	45–60 minutes	3½
Oats (whole groats)	5	2–3 hours	2½
Polenta	5	45–60 minutes	3½
Rye	5	2–3 hours	2
Quinoa	2	20 minutes	2½
Wild rice	3	1–1½ hours	3½
Wheat (whole grain)	5	2–3 hours	2¾
Wheat flakes	2	45–60 minutes	3

NUTS

Quickstart does not use nuts. When buying nuts for Living Lean make sure they are really fresh. The rancid oils in old nuts are harmful to the stomach. They retard pancreatic enzymes and destroy vitamins. If nuts are fresh and whole (unbroken) you can buy a kilo or so at a time and, provided they are kept airtight in a cool dry place (best in the fridge), they will keep for a few months. You can even freeze them and keep them longer. It is a good idea to buy a few different kinds, then if you mix them you will get a good balance of essential amino acids. You will also have more variety in your recipes. Choose from: almonds, Brazils, cashews, coconut (fresh or desiccated), hazels, macadamia nuts, peanuts (strictly speaking a legume), pecans, pine kernels, pistachios, tiger nuts and walnuts.

SEEDS

Except for a smattering of sesame seeds and crushed linseeds Quickstart does not use seeds either. During the Living Lean phase of Go Primitive, be sure you buy really fresh seeds with no signs of decay. The three seeds which provide such a valuable combination of protein and essential fatty acids are sunflower, pumpkin and sesame. Other seeds worth trying, mainly for seasoning, are poppy, celery, caraway, dill, fennel and anise.

LEGUMES

Nutritious, economical and delicious when well prepared, beans and pulses are rich in complex carbohydrates, protein and fibre as well as minerals and essential fatty acids. It is important to know how to handle them and to cook them well in order to avoid digestive upset. All legumes should be washed and cleared of any small pieces of stone or spoilt food. Then everything except lentils, split peas and mung beans should be soaked for at least four to six hours, preferably overnight, before cooking. The soak water should then be thrown away and fresh water should be added. There are two ways to minimize digestive upset when cooking legumes. I use both of them. The first is, after soaking and rinsing, put the legume in the freezer overnight and cook the next day. The second is, after soaking, throw the soak water away, boil up the beans for twenty minutes, throw the boil water away, rinse the beans then put them in more water plus whatever vegetables, herbs and seasonings you may be putting in with them, then cook in a covered saucepan by bringing the beans to a boil, reducing the heat and simmering them until they grow tender. Sprouting is the third way and the most nutritious by far.

There are so many things that you can make with beans that you could fill ten cookbooks with wonderful recipes. I like to make thick soups with them and casseroles. They are great cooked and cold the next day as a base for a wholemeal salad. In either case I add whatever vegetables

GO PRIMITIVE GUIDE TO BEANS AND PULSES

Legume (1 cup)	Soak	Water (cups)	Cooking time (hours)	Yield (cups)
Adzuki	Yes	4	3	2
Baby lima	Yes	3	2	1¾
Black beans	Yes	5	2	2
Cassoulet	Yes	4	3½	2
Chick peas	Yes	4	3½	2½
Kidney	Yes	3	1½	2
Lentils	No	4	1	2¼
Lima	Yes	5	2	1¼
Mung	No	2½	1½	2
Navy	Yes	3	2½	2
Pinto	Yes	3	2½	2
Red	Yes	3	3½	2
Split peas	No	3	1	2¼

I intend to cook with the beans plus some low-salt vegetable broth powder, and whatever other seasoning I am going to use. I then bring the beans to the boil and allow them to simmer for the prescribed length of time. Alternatively, I will bring the beans to the boil and put them in a slow cooker or the bottom of the Aga oven and forget about them for six to eight hours. I sometimes cook beans overnight this way. I soak various kinds of beans, such as lima beans, black-eyed beans, kidney beans, or a mixture of them, pour the soak water away and rinse them, then store them frozen in bags so that I can pull them out whenever I need them to make a casserole or a soup.

Many legumes sprout well, particularly lentils, mung and adzuki beans. Legumes contain a trypsin inhibitor, a substance which blocks the action of some of the enzymes which break down protein in your body, and because of this they must never be eaten raw. Trypsin inhibitors are destroyed when legumes are well cooked. Sprouting also neutralizes them. On page 141 is a chart that will give you some guidelines to the cooking of legumes.

SPROUTS

Seeds and grains are latent powerhouses of nutritional goodness and life energy. Add water to germinate them, let them grow for a few days in your kitchen and you will harvest delicious, inexpensive fresh foods of quite phenomenal health-enhancing value. The vitamin content of seeds increases dramatically when they germinate. There is a huge rise in the levels of vitamin C, A, B-complex, especially B1 and B2, niacin, pantothenic acid, pyridoxine, biotin and folic acid, and in chlorophyll. The vitamin B2 in an oat grain rises by 1,300 per cent almost as soon as the seed sprouts and by the time tiny leaves have formed it has risen by 2,000 per cent. Some sprouted seeds and grains are believed to have anti-cancer properties which is why they form an important part of the gently natural methods of treating the disease.

When you sprout a seed, enzymes which have been dormant in it spring into action breaking down stored starch and turning it into simple natural sugars and splitting long-chain proteins into amino acids. What this means is that the process of sprouting turns these seeds into foods which are very easily assimilated by your body when you eat them. Sprouts are, in effect, pre-digested. As such, they have many times the nutritional efficiency of the seeds from which they have grown. They provide more nutrients gram for gram than any natural food known.

Because of the massive enzyme release which occurs when a seed or grain is sprouted the nutritional quality of a sprout is extremely good. These enzymes not only neutralize such factors as trypsin inhibitors but also destroy other substances which can be harmful, such as phytic acid. Phytic acid, which occurs in considerable quantity in grains, particularly wheat, tends to bind minerals so that the digestive system cannot break them down for assimilation. When a grain is sprouted this mineral-binding capacity is virtually eliminated. Another attractive thing about sprouts is their price. The basic seeds and grains are cheap and readily available in supermarkets and health-food stores – chick peas, brown lentils, mung beans, wheat grains and so forth. And since you sprout them yourself with nothing but clean water, they become an easily accessible source of organically grown fresh vegetables, even for city dwellers. In an age when most vegetables and fruits are grown on artificially fertilized soils and treated with hormones, fungicides, insecticides, preservatives and all manner of other chemicals, the home-grown-in-a-jar sprouts emerge as a pristine blessing – fresh, unpolluted and ready to eat in a minute by popping them into salads or sandwiches.

As such, they can be a wonderful health food not to be ignored by any family concerned about the rising cost of food and the falling nutritional value in the average diet. For they are the cheapest form of natural food around. Different sprouts mixed together will indeed support life all on their own. While I would never suggest that anybody live on sprouts alone, I think they are an ideal addition to the table of every family – particularly if the budget is tight. Children love to help grow them themselves. And because they grow so quickly – the average sprout is ready for the table in about three days – it satisfies their impatience. The youngest member of my family, when he was aged two, used to carry a little bag of sprouts around with him, munching them between meals as some children do sweets.

DIY Sprouting

When you discover how economical and easy it is to grow sprouts you will want to have some on the go all the time. Once germinated you can keep sprouts in polythene bags in the fridge for up to a week – just long enough to get a new batch ready for eating. Most people grow sprouts in glass jars covered with nylon mesh held in place with an elastic band around the neck, but I have discovered an even simpler method which allows you to grow many more and avoids the jar-method problem of seeds rotting due to insufficient drainage. You will need the following:

- Seeds (e.g. mung beans).
- Seed trays with drainage holes, available from gardening shops and nurseries.
- A jar or bowl to soak seeds in overnight.
- A plant atomizer – from gardening or hardware shops.
- A sieve.
- Fine nylon mesh – available from gardening shops.

1. Place two handfuls of seeds or beans in the bottom of a jar or bowl and cover with plenty of water. Leave to soak overnight.

2. Pour the seeds into a sieve and rinse well with water. Be sure to remove any dead or broken seeds or pieces of debris.

3. Line a seedling tray with nylon mesh (this helps the seeds drain better) and pour in the soaked seeds.

4. Place in a warm dark spot for fast growth.

5. Spray the seeds twice a day with fresh water in an atomizer and stir them gently with your hand in order to aerate them.

6. After about three days, place the seeds in sunlight for several hours to develop the chlorophyll (green) in them.

7. Rinse in a sieve, drain well and put in a polythene bag in the fridge to use in salads, wok-frys etc.

There are many different seeds you can sprout – each with its own particular flavour and texture. Use the charts as a guide to the variety of sprouts you can try.

GO PRIMITIVE SPROUTING CHART

Soak time	To yield 1 litre	Ready to eat in	Length of shoot	Growing tips and notes
Alfalfa (6–8 hrs)	3–4 tbsp	5–6 days	3.5cm (1½")	Rich in organic vitamins and minerals, and natural oestrogens.
Fenugreek (6–8 hrs)	½ cup	3–4 days	1cm (½")	Have quite a strong 'curry' taste. Good for ridding the body of toxins.
Adzuki beans (10–15 hrs)	1½ cups	3–5 days	2.5–3.5cm (1–1½")	Have a nutty flavour. Especially good for the kidneys.
Chick peas (10–15 hrs)	2 cups	3–4 days	2.5cm (1")	May need to soak for 18 hrs to swell to their full size. Replace the water during this time.
Lentils (10–15 hrs)	1 cup	3–5 days	0.5–2.5cm (½–1")	Try all different kinds of lentils. They are good eaten young or up to 6 days old
Mung beans (10–15 hrs)	1 cup	3–5 days	1.5cm (½–2½")	Soak at least 15 hours. Keep in the dark for a sweet sprout.
Sunflower (10–15 hrs)	4 cups	1–2 days	same length as grain	Soak them and sprout for just a day. Bruise easily so handle carefully.
Wheat (12–15 hrs)	2 cups	2–3 days	same length as grain	An excellent source of the B vitamins. The soak water can be drunk straight or added to soups and vegetable juices.

SPECIAL FOODS

CAROB (St John's Bread). Carob powder/flour is a superb chocolate substitute – and good for you too. Unlike chocolate it does not contain caffeine. Instead it is full of minerals – calcium, phosphorus, iron, potassium, magnesium and silicon – as well as vitamins B1, B2, niacin and a little vitamin A plus some protein. Carob powder is often sold toasted, but the best kind is raw. It is lighter in colour than the cooked kind. It can be bought from most health-food stores and used to make chocolate drinks, desserts and treats.

AGAR. This starch comes from seaweed. You can use it to make vegetarian gelatine-based sweets and salads and to thicken sauces and topping. It comes in flakes or granules and sometimes in sheets. Soak the agar-agar in a little water to soften it before adding hot liquid to dissolve it. Use about 1 teaspoon to each cup of water or liquid.

ARROWROOT. Made from the pulp of the tuberous rootstocks of a tropical American plant, arrowroot is a nutritious, easily digested food high in calcium. When you heat it in water it thickens (use 1½ teaspoons per cup of liquid). It is better than cornstarch or corn flour to thicken gravy, fruit sauces, soups and stews.

SEA VEGETABLES

If you have never used the sea vegetables for cooking, this is an ideal time to begin. Not only are they delicious – imparting a wonderful, spicy flavour to soups and salads – they are also the richest source of organic mineral salts in nature, particularly of iodine. Iodine is the mineral needed by the thyroid gland. As your thyroid gland is largely responsible for the body's metabolic rate, iodine is very important to a *Lean Revolution*. I like to use powdered kelp as a seasoning. You will find it in some of the recipes. In fact, I use it in many more – it adds both flavour and minerals to salad dressings, salads and soups. I am also very fond of nori seaweed, which comes in long thin sheets. It is a delicious snack food which you can eat along with a salad or at the beginning of the meal: it has a beautiful, crisp flavour. I like to toast it very, very quickly by putting it under a grill for no more than 10 or 15 seconds. It is also delicious raw.

Get to know some of the sea vegetables and start to make use of them. Your nails and hair and the rest of your body will be strengthened by the full range of minerals and trace elements such as selenium, calcium, iodine, boron, potassium, magnesium, iron and others which are not always found in great quantities in our ordinary garden vegetables. You can use nori seaweed to wrap around everything from a sprout salad to cooked grains in order to make little pieces of vegetarian *sushi*. It's often a good idea to soak some of the other sea vegetables such as dulse, arame and hiziki for a few minutes in enough tepid water to cover. This softens them so that they can be easily chopped to be put into salads or added to soups. Sea vegetables are available in health-food stores and in Oriental food shops. Recommended ones are:

- arame
- dulse
- hiziki
- kelp
- kombu
- laver bread
- nori
- wakami

SEASONINGS

MUSTARD. Mustard can be bought in dry or paste form. The dry powder is sometimes useful in dressings. I think the best mustards are French. They are milder and more aromatic than English mustard. Moutarde de Meaux is particularly delicious and is great in dressings for all sorts of salads. Dijon and Bordeaux are also nice.

TAHINI (preferably unroasted). A paste made from ground sesame seeds which is tasty and very nutritious. It has many uses including tahini mayonnaise, and is delicious as an addition to many seed and nut dishes.

LOW-SALT VEGETABLE BOUILLON POWDER. This is something I use a lot to season just about everything. Use it for soup stocks, to flavour pizzas, grains like brown rice and kasha and even salad dressings, stews and casseroles. It is my favourite of all seasonings. The very best is Marigold's Low-Salt Swiss Vegetable Bouillon. I even take it with me when I travel.

YEAST EXTRACT. This can be used as a substitute for vegetable bouillon. It is rich in B-Complex vitamins but very salty, so it should be used in moderation.

FOOD YEAST. This is sometimes called primary yeast or nutritional yeast. It is not brewer's yeast which is a by-product of beer making. Food yeast is grown specifically to be used as a flavouring. It is light yellow-beige and slightly spiky in its texture and is good to add to soups, sauces, cheeses and dips. You can even sprinkle it on popcorn.

VANILLA ESSENCE. Try to find real vanilla essence rather than the more common vanilla flavouring which is synthetic. It gives a delicious warm flavour.

SOYBEAN PRODUCTS

TOFU. Its other name is bean curd. This white, bland soft food made from soybeans is easy to digest, high in protein, low in calories and fat, cheap, and you can use it for just about anything. It behaves a bit like a sponge which will absorb whatever flavour you soak it in. When you cook it, it becomes firmer. You can mix it with herbs, make sauces or low-fat mayonnaise from it, dips for vegetables, pizza toppings and stir-fries. You can even substitute cheese for it in some of your favourite recipes except that it doesn't melt under the grill. Buy it in the supermarket, health-food store or Oriental food shop and keep it sitting in water in the fridge so it doesn't dry out.

MISO. A fermented soybean paste which is rich in digestive enzymes and high in protein. It can be used for seasoning soups and sauces. It is also a delicious addition to dips for crudités and salad dressings.

TAMARI. This is a type of soya sauce made from fermented soybeans, but unlike soya sauce it contains no wheat, although it does contain sea salt so should be used in moderation. It is good for giving a 'Chinese'

taste to dishes as well as a rich flavour to bland dressings or sauces.

SOYA FLOUR. Made from cooked, ground soybeans, soya
flour is sometimes added to grain-based flours to increase
their protein content. It can be used to make soya milk
and soya cheese.

SOYA MILK. Made from cooked, ground and strained
soybeans this is often used for bottle-fed infants who are
allergic to cows' milk. I use it as a substitute for milk on
cereals and in recipes. You can make your own very
cheaply. It's best to make soya milk yourself, if possible,
since the ready-made varieties are packed in aluminium-
lined cartons and this metal can be leached into the soya
milk, as it can into any food that is slightly acidic. Soya
plants themselves appear to have a natural affinity for
aluminium. As part of your diet, it probably makes no
difference. However, it would not be a good idea to base
all your protein on soya as you might risk taking in too
much aluminium.

HERBS

The magicians of Go Primitive cooking, fresh herbs can
transform a humble recipe into a Pasha's delight. I use
them constantly, lavishly, and occasionally with utter aban-
don. I have been known to add as many as seven different
leafy herbs to a simple green salad which becomes more of
a herb salad than a green salad by the time I have finished.
I grow most of my herbs in the garden because there is
something about freshness which you can't re-capture
from the dried varieties. With fresh herbs you needn't
worry much about choosing the wrong ones. Some of my
favourites for salads include lovage (which I also use to
season many salad dressings), basil, dill, the mints, winter
savory, fennel, chives and the parsleys. In the summer I cull
them from the garden. Some I dry by hanging from beams
in the kitchen for a few days and then store them in airtight
jars for winter use. Others – the more succulent herbs
such as parsley, basil and chives – can be deep frozen in

145

sprigs then simply chopped and used when needed. If you live in a flat or don't have a garden, you can grow herbs in pots in the kitchen window where they lend their own beauty to the room as well as offering a constant supply of culinary delights. Thyme, marjoram and winter savory will grow beautifully in pots indoors over the winter. So will parsley. Once you begin to play about with herb magic you will probably find, as I have, that you never want to be without these lovely plants. Here are some of the most common herbs and what I find them useful for.

BASIL. I probably use this herb far too much because it is available only in the summer months and because it is simply so lovely. It has a distinctive flavour which is an ideal garnish for tomatoes or in large amounts mixed into a green salad. Use the leaves whole for the best possible flavour.

CHERVIL. This herb is a cousin to parsley, with a delicate aniseed flavour. We use it lavishly in salads. It mixes particularly well with chives, tarragon and parsley.

CHIVES. More beautiful in looks than in flavour, I think, chives are great for sprinkling on to sunflower wafers or in seed cheeses. I find them not strong enough for most salads and prefer instead spring onions or a little chopped shallots.

DILL. It goes wonderfully with dressings, cucumbers, and beetroot and apple salads, and has a gentle delicate flavour which reminds me of quiet afternoons under sun-shaded willows.

FENNEL. A lacy aniseed-flavoured herb which grows immense in the summer. It goes well with salsify salads and with cucumbers, tomatoes and in vegetable loaves. It is also a lovely decorative herb to place around the edge of a dish of salads.

LOVAGE. Perhaps the most underrated of the common herbs, lovage is wonderful mixed with mints and yoghurt as the base of a herbal salad dressing which is as beautiful in colour as it is in flavour. We also use lots of it in our dish salads.

MARJORAM. This herb comes in many variations – sweet marjoram, pot marjoram, winter marjoram, golden marjoram. Each is a little different. The sweet variety is lovely with plain green salads and goes well with tomatoes and Mediterranean vegetables. Oregano is a wild marjoram akin to our winter variety.

THE MINTS. There are even more varieties than the marjorams – spearmint, peppermint, apple mint, pineapple mint, ginger mint, eau de cologne mint. I use spearmint and apple mint in green salads and many dressings. Pineapple mint, with its splendid variegated leaves, makes a wonderful garnish for fruit salads, drinks and also salad platters. Ginger mint is great in summer drinks, sorbets and punches.

PARSLEY. This common herb comes in two main varieties – fine and broad leaf. For most raw dishes we prefer the broadleaf parsley because it is more delicate and pleasant to munch. Both have a rich 'green' flavour which works well with other herbs. It is great chopped in patties and loaves, in green salads and for dressings, as well as being a lovely garnish for almost any dish.

SAGE. This herb has a strong individual flavour and a particular affinity for onions. It is good in savoury nut dishes and adds flavour to seed and nut ferments.

THYME. It comes in many varieties, some of which are much richer in flavour than others, but all have a wonderful warming sweet flavour which enhances peppers, courgettes and nut dishes as well as giving a unique flavour to sprout salads.

THE LEAN REVOLUTION KITCHEN

The mainstay of my kitchen is not the hob or the oven but the food processor. It is the one piece of equipment I would never want to do without. And because I have such a large family we have one of the big varieties which holds twice the ordinary quantity of soups, vegetables, nuts and seeds. For although most of the recipes that follow can be made by hand, the addition of a food processor to your kitchen equipment is such a boon in the time and energy it saves (you can prepare a whole salad meal in about five minutes), that it would be a pity to have to do without one – particularly if you are preparing food for more than two people.

A SIMPLE PROCESSOR. There are many different models on the market, most of which I have tried, and some of which I have found completely infuriating. Processors vary enormously in their convenience of use as well as their durability. When buying a food processor it is best to choose the simplest one you can find. Those big all-purpose kitchen machines which do everything are not only a pain to put together, take apart and clean, but you are for ever hunting for some little part you need for what you are doing when you could have your soup, salad or muesli already finished. Each machine comes with several attachments. There is a blade which is excellent for grinding nuts and seeds, homogenizing vegetables for soups and loaves, and making dressings, dips and sweets. The grater (some come with two – a coarse and a fine) is ideal for fruit when making muesli or for some salads, the slicer for other salads and desserts. Most food processors also have a pastry attachment – a little white plastic blade which I have always found totally useless even for making pastry. The ordinary blade does everything better.

BLENDER AID. A blender, too, can be helpful for grinding nuts and seeds – provided you supply yourself with something like a chopstick to clear the blade when you are blending dry ingredients. If you have to choose between a blender and a processor, go for the processor, since you can do everything in it you can do in a blender. But if you are fortunate enough to have both you will probably find that the blender is easier to use for drinks while the processor works better for everything else. Even a coffee grinder can be useful for grinding small quantities of nuts if you have nothing else.

SLOW COOKER. If you are lucky enough to have an Aga or another kind of old-fashioned country cooker which is

148

always hot and has a slow oven, this is great for making thick soups, stews and casseroles. You simply start them on the top of the stove and then pop them into the slow oven and forget them for many hours or even overnight – a great way to make porridge and other cooked cereals that are instantly ready for breakfast. If not, consider investing in a slow cooker. These little gems are ideal for doing the same things. It consists of a big casserole dish in a rather ugly (usually nondescript beige) base which plugs into the mains yet uses about the same electricity that a light bulb does to cook your grains and stews, cereals and puddings the way that great-grandmother did – slow and perfect without ever burning. I do have an Aga but I use my slow cooker often nonetheless. They are a good investment and a real time-saver since you can prepare a big meal way ahead of time and return home to find it perfectly cooked.

POTS AND PANS. Get hold of some good non-stick cookware if you can. The heavier the better. You can use them to sauté with no oil without your food sticking – maybe a big saucepan, a lidded skillet or crêpe pan and a couple of baking dishes and baking sheets. A steamer can also be helpful for vegetables as can a *bain marie* or what in America is called a double boiler. I recently bought a great contraption which is a heavy cast-iron enamelled Le Creuset pot which came with two attachments – a steamer and a bain-marie top which sit over it – plus a lid. I bought it on impulse because it looked curious but ever since then hardly a day goes by without my using it for one thing or another – including rinsing pasta and sprouted grains. I recommend it highly. A wok is also useful for stir-frying and steaming.

HAND HELP. There are some useful little mechanical gadgets which can be enormously useful to the Go Primitive cook. For instance, the Swiss, the French and the Dutch have well-designed food mills for grating and chopping which you can use instead of a food processor to shred vegetables and fruits. But when buying one

149

make sure it comes apart easily, has stainless-steel blades and is simple to clean. We often use an ordinary stainless-steel grater for making bowls of muesli or for grating cheese. The reason for the stainless steel is that it does not oxidize and therefore does not destroy vitamin C in the foods you are shredding as do many of the other metals.

A GOOD EDGE. Several sharp knives in different sizes and a couple of good chopping boards are indispensable to the Go Primitive chef. Here I break my stainless-steel rule simply because you can get a much better edge on a carbon steel knife. A knife sharpener is an absolute must. Another little gadget I use a lot is a salad washer – a basket in which you can spin your washed lettuce leaves to dry them before turning them into a seductive salad. Steer clear of anything made of aluminium that could come in contact with food such as tomatoes. Aluminium oxide tends to form which, when repeatedly taken into the body with the foods, can cause the serious symptoms of aluminium poisoning.

CHILL OUT. Finally the thing you need most for fresh foods, unless you are going to be cutting your lettuces from the garden one moment and popping them into salads the next, is a refrigerator. I tend to wash many of my vegetables as soon as I get them home before putting them into vegetable bins in the fridge. This means than when I go down to the kitchen to prepare a meal they are all freshly clean and waiting for me.

SHEER INDULGENCE. My big passion at breakfast is waffles. They are the easiest thing in the world to make and completely delicious spread with a fruit jam or topping. And children adore them. To make them you need a waffle iron and these are not cheap but they make a great gift next time somebody asks you what you want for Christmas. I prepare the batter ahead of time (sometimes I even freeze it in packets just the right size for breakfast and then defrost it overnight). You can also make them ahead of time and pop them in a toaster for a nourishing quick breakfast for kids.

Recipes

BREAKFAST

Breakfast is the most important meal of the day – between one-third and a half of your calories on Go Primitive should come from breakfast alone. A hearty breakfast full of complex carbohydrates provides you with nutrient-rich fuel to keep you going for five or six hours. It may take a week or two to get used to eating a good breakfast and reducing the size of your evening meal, but you will soon be surprised at how your energy levels improve along with your general mood. Eating a good breakfast also helps get rid of any elimination problems. It takes time if you are not eating breakfast to make the change. Try eating dinner earlier in the day, and make dinner a lighter and lighter meal. Eventually you may want to skip dinner altogether. This makes breakfast an enormous pleasure, eaten when you are very hungry. It also improves the quality of sleep. Many people find that they need less sleep as the sleep that they are getting is so much more restful.

Remember to drink a couple of glasses of pure water as soon as you wake up. This helps prime your digestive juices for breakfast when it comes. Here are some of my breakfast recipes. Try to vary the varieties of grain that you eat throughout the week in your toasts, mueslis, cereals, porridge or baked breakfasts. This way you get a full complement of the various minerals and other nutrients. The more variety the better.

Raisin & Oat Porridge

Porridge can be made the night before in a thermos, in the bottom of an Aga or in a slow cooker, by pouring boiling water over the other ingredients and simply allowing it to sit at a low heat all night. That way, even if you are in a hurry in the morning, you have an instant hot breakfast. This is a favourite with athletes.

½ cup raisins	*1 tablespoon concentrated apple*
1½ cups rolled oats	*or pear juice*
1 teaspoon cinnamon	*6 cups boiling water*
	nutmeg

Either: place all ingredients in a saucepan and bring to the boil, simmering until all the water has been absorbed. This can take 20 minutes. Serve with a little grated nutmeg.

Or: put all ingredients into a thermos, pour boiling water over them and leave overnight.

Or: cook overnight in a slow cooker or the bottom oven of an aga. You can vary the porridge you make by using other grain flakes such as barley, wheat, millet, brown rice and rye.

Raw Muesli

This recipe, which is my family's very favourite breakfast, calls for an apple, but you can use almost any fruit – strawberries, peaches, apricots, cherries, even unsulphured dried fruits (but be sure to soak them overnight in spring water so that they plump up). Choose whatever fruit is inexpensive and in season.

The recipe serves 1, but can just as easily be made for 12. This particular form of muesli is dairy-free but if you prefer to use dairy products you can use plain low-fat yoghurt in place of soya milk. The grains are soaked overnight so that enzymes break down the hard-to-digest starches making them much sweeter and much easier to absorb.

2 tablespoons of oat flakes, or a	*juice of ½ lemon*
combination of oat, rye, wheat	*3 tablespoons soya milk or low-fat*
etc., soaked overnight in a little	*yoghurt*
spring water or fruit juice	*1 tablespoon of concentrated*
A handful of raisins also	*apple, pear or strawberry juice*
soaked overnight	*½ teaspoon of powdered*
1 apple or pear, grated	*cinnamon or ginger*

Mix together the soaked oat flakes and raisins and combine this mixture with the grated apple or pear, lemon juice and the soya milk, or low-fat yoghurt if you prefer. Drizzle with fruit juice and sprinkle with cinnamon or ginger. Serve immediately. Here are a few variations on raw muesli to inspire you.

Winter Muesli
Soak a selection of dried fruit overnight in spring water. Dice into small pieces or cut up with scissors and add to the soaked grain flakes. Add the lemon juice, yoghurt or soya milk and concentrated fruit juice. Spice with a little grated nutmeg.

Fruit Juice Muesli
Substitute the soya milk or yoghurt for some fresh fruit juice such as apple, orange or grape. To thicken the juice blend with a little fresh fruit in season such as banana, pear or apple.

Banana Muesli
Add a banana sliced in quarters lengthwise and then chopped crosswise into small pieces, or mash a banana with a little soya milk, yoghurt or fruit juice and use it as a topping.

Summer Muesli
Add a handful of raisins, strawberries, blackcurrants or pitted cherries to the basic muesli, or substitute the apple for a finely diced peach or nectarine.

Blended Muesli
For young children or the elderly it is a good idea to blend all the muesli ingredients together in a food processor. This gives a nourishing and delicious purée which requires no chewing.

Breakfast Crêpes *(Living Lean only)*
This mixture improves if it is made the night before and left to stand in the fridge before cooking. It is fat-free.

1 cup rolled oats	*2 tablespoons shredded coconut*
1½ cups wholewheat flour	*4 cups soya milk*
1 cup oat bran	*2 tablespoons concentrated*
½ teaspoon ground coriander	*fruit juice (apple or pear)*
(optional)	*2 teaspoons vanilla essence*

Blend all the ingredients together until smooth. Let the batter stand for 5 minutes then blend again. Oil a frying pan or griddle with a little extra virgin oil or cold-pressed soya oil. Heat the pan then pour the oil off. Pour out ⅓ cup of batter for each crêpe and wait until bubbles appear and turn over. Cook until golden brown on both sides and serve with a fruit topping, or roll them around some fresh fruit. You may also spread a little nut butter on the crêpes and roll around some chopped banana.

As a variation you can substitute corn meal for the rolled oats and toss in ½ a cup of sesame seeds.

Or: replace the oat bran with the same amount of fresh or frozen raspberries, strawberries or blueberries.

Feather-light Waffles

Most whole-grain waffles are as heavy as bricks because they use too much whole grain wheat flour. These, however, are heavenly light. They are great spread with hazelnut or cashew butter when you are Living Lean, or topped with date butter, apple butter or one of the fruit toppings during Quickstart. You can even mash a very ripe banana with a little concentrated fruit juice and spread it on. The coconut is optional but adds something extra special when you are Living Lean. Do use baking powder or bicarbonate of soda if you like. Personally, I prefer not to as it can interfere with the assimilation of vitamins.

2 cups rolled oats	½ teaspoon cinnamon or nutmeg
3 tablespoons shredded coconut	2 cups soya milk
(optional)	2 teaspoons vanilla essence
½ teaspoon ground coriander	pinch of salt

Heat up a non-stick waffle iron. Blend all the ingredients together until creamy. Pour in enough waffle mixture to cover the iron and shut the lid. Leave to cook (without opening) until the waffle stops steaming – about 7–10 minutes. Be prepared to experiment and burn the odd one. Serve with a fruit topping or fresh fruit.

Munchy-Crunchy Granola

An excellent make-it-ahead dried cereal that you can keep in the fridge for instant breakfast. It uses a mixture of grains. For Quickstart, omit the seeds since they are high in fat, or cut the quantities way down. This recipe makes approximately 30 servings and will keep, tightly closed in the refrigerator, for a couple of weeks. You can shift the percentage of flakes, depending on what you have in the larder.

5 cups of steel-cut or rolled oats	2 teaspoons of freshly grated
1 cup of oat bran	nutmeg
1 cup of barley flakes	2 cups pitted dates
1 cup of wheat flakes	1½ cups fruit juice concentrate
½ cup of rye flakes	(try apple, pear, apricot, or
½ cup sliced almonds	tropical fruit) or 300 g (12oz)
2 cups shredded, unsweetened	tin unsweetened concentrated
coconut	pineapple juice
½ cup sunflower seeds	1 teaspoon of ground coriander
½ cup raw sesame seeds	1 teaspoon salt
1 tablespoon of ground	1 cup raisins
cinnamon	

Mix the grains and seeds and almonds together. Place the dates, fruit juice and all the other ingredients except the raisins in a food processor and mix until creamy. Add the fruit cream to the dry ingredients and mix with your hands in a large bowl. Spread the mixture on 3 large baking tins, about 2.5 cm (1 in) thick, and put into a 170°C (325°F) Gas 3 oven. Allow to cook for 2 to 3 hours, stirring every half hour. After the granola has cooled, take it from the baking sheet and mix in the raisins. Store in airtight containers in a cool place.

A variation on this is that after the granola is cooked but before you add the raisins, put the dry toasted mixture into a food processor and blend into small bits. This makes a very crunchy, delicious dry cereal with a different texture to which you can add a bit of fruit.

You can substitute pecans, walnuts or hazelnuts for the almonds.

Baked Breakfast Pudding

This recipe is baked in the oven for 45 minutes before breakfast, or you can make it ahead and serve it cold with sliced bananas, date butter or apple butter as a topping, plus a little soya milk or skimmed milk. Serves 4.

2 large apples, chopped
2 cups of cooked brown rice
½ cup raisins or dried,
*   unsulphured apricots, preferably*
*   soaked in 1 cup of apple juice*
*   or spring water*

2 ripe bananas
½ cup date butter
2 teaspoons vanilla essence
¾ cup of concentrated
*   frozen orange juice*
*   or other fruit juice concentrate*

Mix the chopped apples, brown rice and raisins together. Blend the other ingredients in a food processor and stir into the apple–rice mixture. Bake for 45 minutes at 180°C (350°F) Gas 4.

Scrambled Tofu

Scrambled tofu is great on whole-grain rye toast. It is an excellent alternative to scrambled eggs for Sunday brunch.

½ cup diced onions
½ cup diced carrots
½ cup chopped celery
2 cloves garlic
1 teaspoon olive or soya oil

2 cups mashed, drained tofu
1 tablespoon soy sauce
2 teaspoons low-salt vegetable
*   bouillon powder or food yeast*
1 teaspoon mild curry powder

Sauté onions, carrots, celery and garlic in a heavy frying pan using the olive or soya oil. When brown, add the tofu, soy sauce, low-salt vegetable bouillon and curry powder. Stir together over a medium heat for 5–10 minutes. Delicious served with oven-fried chips.

Cracked Wheat Cereal

Toast wheat grains in a slow oven for an hour, stirring occasionally. Put them into a food processor and mince them. This can be done ahead of time. You can do the same thing with whole rye, oats or brown rice.

1 cup minced wheat	*pinch of salt*
½ cup seeded dates, chopped	*4 cups spring water*

Put all ingredients into a pan, bring to the boil and simmer for about 20 minutes until soft. Cracked wheat is an excellent alternative to porridge.

Raisin Bran Muffins

These muffins are yummy and sweet thanks to the concentrated pear juice. You can also make them with concentrated apple juice or even water.

3 cups finely milled wheat flour	*1½ cups oat or wheat bran*
1 teaspoon ground cinnamon	*1 cup raisins*
½ teaspoon grated nutmeg	*3 cups chopped apples*
2 teaspoons baking powder	*½ cup concentrated pear*
(optional)	*or apple juice mixed with*
½ teaspoon grated coriander	*1 cup of water*

Sift the flour and spices with the baking powder if you choose to use it. Add the oat bran, raisins and chopped apples. Add the fruit juice and water and mix well. Spoon the mixture into non-stick muffin tins and bake in a 170°C (325°F) Gas 3 oven for 20–30 minutes. As a variation use dates or apricots with the apples.

MAIN MEALS

These recipes are designed to form the core of a main meal which is best eaten at lunchtime or before 4 o'clock in the afternoon when your body handles energy most efficiently without turning it into fat. My favourite main meals are usually based around soups or casseroles that are prepared in advance and cooked slowly, but a main meal can be a pizza or a grain dish with vegetables or even a delicious shepherd's pie.

Serve your main dish together with a good salad or a bowl of sprouted seeds and grains, and some whole-grain bread served with a spread or jam. Do include green vegetables, either in salad or as cooked vegetables. Most important, give yourself plenty of time to eat and do enjoy the ritual. There is little that helps you handle stress better than sitting down to a delicious meal and allowing yourself to enjoy it.

Easy Vegetable Curry

This is a simple and yet delicious dish which takes no more than 20–30 minutes to prepare. It is a good dish to be eaten on its own or with a light salad for supper. In smaller quantities it can be served as a side-dish to go with a large salad.

1 large onion, finely chopped
1 teaspoon olive oil
2 teaspoons mild curry powder
3 large carrots, sliced three or
*   four times lengthways, then*
*   cut across to make 4-cm*
*   (1½-in) sticks*

1 medium-sized turnip, cut
*   up finely into matchsticks*
2 potatoes, cut up into chunks
1–1½ teaspoons low-salt
*   vegetable bouillon powder*
1½ cups spring water
grated coconut (optional)

Sauté the onion in the oil until it becomes translucent, then add the curry powder and vegetable bouillon powder and continue to stir for a few minutes. Add the rest of the vegetables and pour in the water. Bring to the boil and simmer slowly for 20–30 minutes then serve. It is particularly nice served with some grated dried coconut.

This vegetable curry can be adapted to whatever vegetables you have on hand. During the summer it's delightful to be able to add some French beans or perhaps some peas,or chopped celery.

Burgers

Here are a couple of my favourite recipes for burgers. I spent my childhood in America where burgers are king. I adore putting them together with Go Primitive ingredients and stacking them high on whole-grain hamburger buns full of tomato slices, pimento cheese and onions, and all the other delicious condiments in their low-fat form.

4 whole-grain hamburger
*   buns, halved*
4 burgers (see Burger Mix)
4 thick slices of tomato
1 cup tofu mayonnaise or

pimento cashew cheese
4 slices red onions
4 lettuce leaves
¾ cup alfalfa sprouts
*   (optional)*

Spread the buns lavishly with the mayonnaise and layer the other ingredients including the burgers on top to make as thick a sandwich as you can manage and still get your teeth round it – my number 1 favourite.

Burger Mix

You can make burgers from just about any leftovers of pulses that you have got – lima beans, black-eyed peas, kidney beans or chick peas. Here's how.

2 cups mashed beans or pulses
1 cup crumbled breadcrumbs
2 tablespoons chick pea flour or
  fine wheat flour
1 onion, minced
2 tablespoons low-salt vegetable

bouillon powder
2 tablespoons Worcester sauce
2 cloves garlic, mashed or
  chopped fine
1 teaspoon sage

Blend the cooked pulses until smooth. Pour into a bowl and add the other ingredients (except the breadcrumbs). Shape into patties. Roll in seasoned breadcrumbs and either bake for 45 minutes in a 190°C (375°F) Gas 5 oven or cook in a non-stick frying pan until golden brown on both sides.

Oat Burgers

These burgers are rich, munchy and delicious and belong to the Living Lean phase of Go Primitive. I like to make them in large quantities and freeze them so that they are ready to use whenever I need them.

2 cups water
2 tablespoons Worcester sauce
½ cup pecans or walnuts, chopped
4 tablespoons low-salt vegetable
  bouillon powder
3 cloves garlic, crushed – or
  1 tablespoon garlic powder

1 tablespoon dried sweet basil, or
  a handful of fresh basil
3 tablespoons fresh parsley,
  chopped
1 tablespoon onion powder
½ teaspoon ground coriander
½ teaspoon dried sage
2 cups steel-cut oats

Put all the ingredients except the oats into a large pan and bring to a slow boil over a medium heat. Remove from heat, add the oats and leave to cool. Form the mixture into 7.5 cm (3 in) patties and bake on a non-stick baking sheet, 15 minutes per side, in a 180°C (350°F) Gas 4 oven.

Dahl Stew

I make this either with red lentils or dried yellow split peas. It has a curry flavour but contains coarsely chopped vegetables.

¾–1 cup red lentils or split peas
1 large cauliflower, broken into
  florets
3 large carrots, cut into chunky
  pieces

pinch of turmeric
3 cloves garlic, chopped
2 tablespoons low-salt vegetable
  bouillon powder
1 large onion, finely chopped

1 sweet red pepper, chopped
1 sweet yellow pepper, chopped
2 teaspoons ground cumin
2 teaspoons coriander
2 tablespoons fresh ginger, finely
   chopped

1–2 teaspoons mild curry powder
1 large parsnip, cut into pieces
1 cup broccoli florets
2 large tomatoes, chopped or
   3 tablespoons of tomato paste
   with ½ cup water

Put the red lentils or split peas into a large pot and cover with 3 cups water and 1 tablespoon low-salt vegetable bouillon powder. Cook for 45 minutes until tender. Purée in a food processor and set them aside. While the peas are cooking, braise the onion in a little water with the garlic, turmeric, ginger and 1 tablespoon vegetable bouillon. When they have softened add the vegetables, except the broccoli, and other seasonings and simmer until cooked. Pour the puréed legume mixture into the vegetables, add the broccoli and serve immediately.

Chilli

Chilli is one of my favourite dishes. I like to make it thick and eat it with slabs of rich dark bread or corn bread. I also like to purée it and use it the next day to make burgers.

2 cups dry kidney beans
4 sticks celery, chopped
1 small onion, chopped
3 tablespoons tinned tomatoes
   in their juice
3 garlic cloves, minced
½ cup green peppers, chopped
2 tablespoons low-salt vegetable
   bouillon powder

2 teaspoons cumin
1 tablespoon chilli powder
3 sprigs fresh marjoram
   (when available)
3 tablespoons concentrated
   apple juice
½ cup tomato paste
2 teaspoons olive oil
2 tablespoons spring water

Soak the beans overnight, rinse and drain. Put into a pan and cover with spring water – about 5 cm (2 in) above the beans. Bring to the boil and simmer until tender. Sauté the garlic, peppers and onion in the olive oil then add the remaining ingredients and stir well. Add this mixture to the kidney beans when they are cooked, re-adjusting the water as necessary and simmer for another hour. Serve hot with warmed chunks of bread.

Pizza

This is a basic recipe for a pizza which you can, of course, adapt as you like. There are so many delicious toppings you could go on experimenting forever.

Pizza base:
3 cups finely ground wheat flour
1 teaspoon salt
1 tablespoon yeast
1 cup spring water (warmed
   to activate the yeast)

Pizza sauce:
1 cup tomato purée
¼ cup apple concentrate
juice of 1 lemon
2 teaspoons low-salt vegetable
   bouillon powder
1 clove garlic, crushed
¼ teaspoon oregano
1 teaspoon salt

Topping:
Pizza sauce
1 cup mushrooms
2 large tomatoes, sliced
a handful of pitted olives
   (optional)
1 green pepper, sliced
1 yellow pepper, sliced
2 cloves garlic, cut into slivers
1 red onion, finely sliced
4–5 fresh basil leaves, finely
   chopped
½ teaspoon oregano
½ teaspoon thyme
freshly ground black pepper

Stir the yeast into the water and allow to stand for 15 minutes until the water has a thin layer of bubbles. Add the yeast mixture to the flour and salt and knead (in a processor if you can) until you have a firm ball. Knead for another 10 minutes by hand, adding more flour if the dough is too sticky. Put the dough in a bowl draped with a tea-towel and leave in a warm place for 45 minutes, or until the dough has doubled in size. Push it back down to get rid of some of the air and knead again for just 1 minute. Pull the dough out into a circle with your fingers, making sure it is thicker at the edges than in the middle. Lightly flour a baking tray and put the pizza base on it.

Make your pizza sauce by putting all the ingredients in a food processor and blending well. If it is too thick add a little water. Spread the sauce over the uncooked pizza base.

Arrange your choice of topping over the pizza base and choose anything else your imagination inspires you to use. Cook in a hot oven for 15 minutes or until the crust has browned.

SOUPS

Some of my recipes for soups that you will find listed here are conventional soups that you could well serve together with a main course and salad. However, many of them are so rich and hearty they are a full meal in themselves. I adore peasant soups. Years ago I teased my children when they expressed particular admiration of a thick lentil soup that I had prepared. It was November. I told them that they could expect nothing but soup to eat until Easter. They laughed, thinking that I was joking but in reality it turned out to be just about true. We all became so enthusiastic about preparing soups and experimented with so many different varieties of soups and gruels that, apart from our salads and breakfasts, they formed the core of everything we did eat that winter. It was a winter of exploration into the soup realm that I have never forgotten and from which I learned a great deal. I can't recommend soups highly enough.

Curried Pumpkin Soup
This soup is spicy and goes beautifully with a sprout salad.

2 medium onions, finely chopped
1 clove garlic, finely chopped
2 cups fresh pumpkin, cubed
   (or marrow, if you prefer)
1 teaspoon olive oil
3 cups water, boiled
200 g (7 oz) mushrooms, sliced
½ teaspoon ground cumin
½ teaspoon coriander
½ teaspoon cinnamon
½ teaspoon ground ginger
teaspoon mustard powder
2 teaspoons low-salt vegetable
   bouillon powder
juice of 2 lemons
½ teaspoon mustard powder

Sauté the onions, the garlic, the pumpkin and the mushrooms in olive oil until soft. Add the boiled water and cook for 10 minutes. Add seasonings and cook for another 5 to 10 minutes. Place in a blender or food processor and blend thoroughly. Add freshly squeezed lemon juice and serve.

Corn Soup
This soup is uncooked and can either be served cold or hot.

2 fresh corn on the cob
300 ml (½ pint) warm spring
   water
2 spring onions
1 teaspoon low-salt vegetable
   bouillon powder
¼ red pepper, chopped
¼ green pepper, chopped
1 tablespoon watercress, finely
   chopped
1 tablespoon tahini (optional)

Wash the corn and cut the kernels off the cob with a knife. Mix together with the water, spring onions and vegetable bouillon powder, season with tahini (if desired) and blend until creamy in a blender or food processor. Add the chopped peppers and watercress to each portion.

Split Pea Soup
This is a filling soup, quite heavy, which goes wonderfully well with a sprout or green salad.

161

1 cup dried split peas, soaked in spring water overnight	1 litre (1¾ pints) spring water
1 large onion, chopped	1 tablespoon low-salt vegetable bouillon powder
2 medium carrots, diced	2 tablespoons chopped fresh herbs as available
2 sticks of celery, diced	

After the peas have been washed and soaked overnight, put them in a pot with all the vegetables and cover with water. Bring to the boil and simmer for 1½ hours until the peas are tender. Add the vegetable bouillon and fresh herbs 5 minutes before serving. If you want a smooth soup, put into a food processor or blender and process.

Thick Vegetable Soup

This makes enough for a good 4 to 6 servings.

4 carrots	1 teaspoon olive oil
2 turnips	1 tablespoon low-salt vegetable bouillon powder
2 leeks	
1 head celery	2 bay leaves
1 parsnip	1.5 litres (2½ pints) spring water
2 cups garden peas	¾ cup brown rice or millet
1 cup runner beans, chopped	fresh parsley, chopped

Wash and scrub the vegetables. Cut the root vegetables into small cubes, the leeks first lengthwise 4 to 6 times, then across, so you get tiny pieces. Add the oil to the pot and sauté the leeks. Then add chopped celery, carrots and turnips, putting the lid on to allow them to sweat for 5 minutes. Now add the vegetable bouillon, bay leaves, stock or water (boiling) and the rice, and allow to cook for 30 minutes. Now add peas and beans and cook for another 15 minutes. Sprinkle with chopped parsley and serve.

Luscious Lentil Soup

This soup is not really a soup at all but a main course. It, like many of the soups I like best, are like gruels – enormously nourishing after long walks in the hills or on a dark winter's day.

400 g (14 oz) dried lentils	(unsulphured)
4 medium carrots, chopped	2 parsnips, chopped
6 sticks celery, chopped	2–3 tablespoons low-salt vegetable bouillon powder
200 g (7 oz) small white potatoes, halved lengthwise	
2–3 leeks, the white part	½ teaspoon dried sage
1 large onion, chopped	½ teaspoon dried thyme
3–4 chopped tomatoes or a small tin of tomatoes	4 cloves garlic, crushed
	juice of ½ a lemon
1 tablespoon black molasses	freshly ground black pepper
	freshly chopped parsley

Wash the lentils, place in a large pot and cover with 5–7.5 cm
(2 – 3 in) of water. Bring to the boil. Add the remaining ingredients (exept lemon juice and parsley) and simmer for 45 minutes.
I generally bring the soup to the boil and then put it into the aga
and just let it sit for 45 minutes. Add lemon juice and parsley just
before serving.

GRAINS

Here are some grain dishes that can themselves be the basis
of a main meal served together with a salad or vegetables.
Grains are particularly good for athletes since they are the
lightest form of complex carbohydrates to release energy
slowly over many hours while you work or exercise. Each
grain has its own natural characteristic. The important thing
is to vary the grains that you eat, for each grain also has its
own synergistic complements of vitamins and minerals.

Yummy Brown Rice

Rice cooked in this manner is so delicious that it seems to be a
worthwhile dish in itself. It needs no special sauces or condiments
to make it work.

1 cup brown rice
2–3 cups spring water
2 teaspoons vegetable bouillon
* powder*

3 tablespoons fresh parsley,
* chopped*
1 teaspoon marjoram
2 cloves garlic, finely chopped
* (optional)*

Wash the rice 3 times under running water and put into a saucepan.
Boil the water in a kettle and pour over the rice. Add seasonings
except for the parsley. Bring to the boil and cook gently for 45
minutes or until all the liquid has been absorbed. Garnish with
parsley and serve. If you double the quantities used here you can
keep some back and make a delicious rice salad the next day.

Kasha

Kasha has been a favourite for me ever since a Russian lover taught
me how to make this traditional dish. It makes a wonderful breakfast – especially to share in bed on a Sunday morning.

2 cups buckwheat groats
spring water to cover
2 teaspoons low-salt vegetable
* bouillon powder*

2 tablespoons fresh parsley or
* other herbs, chopped*
1 clove of garlic, crushed

Place the buckwheat in a heavy-bottomed pan and roast it dry over a medium heat while stirring with a wooden spoon. As it begins to darken, pour hot water over it and add the vegetable bouillon powder, garlic and 1 teaspoon of the herbs. Cover and simmer very slowly for about 15–20 minutes until all the liquid has been absorbed. Serve sprinkled with the remaining herbs or pour a light gravy over the top.

Polenta

Polenta is a dish made from cornmeal. I particularly like it served with a salad dressed with a spicy sauce.

3 cups spring water	2 teaspoons low-salt vegetable
1 cup cornmeal	bouillon powder

Heat the water in a kettle. Pour boiling water over the cornmeal and blend into a paste with the vegetable bouillon powder. Stir until smooth and cook very gently until all the liquid has been absorbed. Cool and drop by the spoonful on to a very lightly oiled baking sheet and grill until brown, turning once.

Barley Pilaff

A delicious baked dish. It is made from pot barley not from pearl barley. Barley is also excellent used in soups.

2 onions, finely chopped	1 tablespoon low-salt vegetable
1 teaspoon olive oil	bouillon powder
1 cup pot barley	1 tablespoon dill
1½ cups spring water	2 cloves of garlic, finely chopped (optional)

Sauté the onions in the oil until translucent, then add the barley to the pan and stir well. Remove from the heat and add the remaining ingredients (including the water, boiled in a kettle). Place in a lightly oiled oven dish and bake in a moderate oven for half an hour. Check to see if you need to add a little more water. Serve immediately.

VEGETABLES

Vegetables have become the most neglected of all natural foods in the last half-century and it is a pity because the colour, texture and variety of flavours they offer is quite remarkable. As you vary the grains, try also to vary the vegetables. The best way to cook vegetables is either to steam them or to wok fry them in a teaspoon of olive or sesame oil. Don't over-cook them or you will ruin their flavour and cause them to lose their colour. Here are a few of my favourite vegetable dishes.

Artichokes
Artichokes are one of my favourite vegetables. I like them served in almost any form. A simple vinaigrette sauce is perhaps best of all.

4 large artichokes
juice of ½ lemon

sea salt to taste
vinaigrette sauce

Place the artichokes in a large pot of boiling water – at least 7.5 cm (3 in) depth of water. Add the lemon juice and a pinch or two of sea salt to season, and bring to the boil. Simmer for 45 minutes until the meat at the bottom of each artichoke leaf is softened. Remove and serve either hot or cold with a simple vinaigrette sauce.

Minty Peas
400 g (14 oz) fresh shelled
garden peas
½ teaspoon vegetable bouillon
powder

1 tablespoon spring water
2 tablespoons fresh mint (apple
mint is particularly good)

Put the peas into a pot with the water and vegetable bouillon powder and gently steam over a low heat for 15–20 minutes. Sprinkle with the mint for the last 5 minutes of cooking and serve immediately.

Pumpkin in Tahini
The small amount of tahini used here sets the pumpkin off nicely.

1 large onion, finely chopped
1 teaspoon olive oil
1 tablespoon tahini

400 g (14 oz) fresh pumpkin,
skin removed and cubed
½ teaspoon nutmeg, grated

Sauté the onion in the oil until brown, then add the pumpkin and continue to sauté for 15–20 minutes, stirring carefully. Add a splash of water if necessary and leave on a very low heat for another 10–15 minutes, until soft. Add the tahini and mix well. Serve immediately sprinkled with the grated nutmeg.

Jacket Potatoes
Baked potatoes make the most wonderful 'pockets' for salads, steamed vegetables, dips and so forth. What you need to avoid are the traditional cheese, sour cream, yoghurt etc. baked-potato fillings because they are too high in fat.

Baked Carrots

6 large carrots　　　*¼ cup sesame seeds*
1 teaspoon olive oil

Scrub the carrots well and slice them lengthways 4 or 5 times, then crosswise into pieces about 7.5 cm (3 in) long. Mix well with the oil, then place on a baking sheet and bake in a hot oven for 20 minutes. During the last 10 minutes of baking sprinkle the sesame seeds over the top. Serve immediately.

Baked Parsnips

The sweetness of parsnips always surprises me. Full of fibre and delicious, they are one of my favourite vegetables. This is an easy way to get the best from them.

400 g (14 oz) fresh parsnips　　*½ teaspoon vegetable bouillon*
3 tablespoons of concentrated　　　*powder*
*　fruit juice or 1 teaspoon olive oil*　*2 tablespoons Dijon mustard*

Slice the parsnips lengthways 2 or 3 times, then crosswise into lengths about 7.5 cm (3 in) long. Mix together the fruit concentrate or oil, the vegetable bouillon powder and the mustard, and pour over to cover the parsnips using a tablespoon or two of water in the mixture if you need it. Bake in a moderate oven until golden brown – about 30–35 minutes.

Cottage Fried Potatoes

These are a great replacement for chips or french fries. Kids love them. Once they get used to living without all the grease, most come to like them even better than the conventional variety.

6 medium potatoes　　　*1 tablespoon onion salt*
1 tablespoon garlic salt　　*2 tablespoons finely milled*
*　　　　　　　　　　　　　whole-grain flour*

Scrub the potatoes thoroughly, leaving the skins on. Cut them lengthways in strips or put them through a food processor using the chipper attachment. Mix the garlic salt and onion salt with the flour. Sprinkle through the potatoes (their dampness will pick up a fine coating of the flour mixture). Place on a non-stick baking sheet and bake for 30–40 minutes at 230°C (450°F) Gas 8.

Ginger Sweet Potatoes

Sweet potatoes or yams are very high in fibre and the starches and sugars they contain are much more slowly absorbed into the system than with ordinary potatoes. I like the yams that are bright orange inside, but they are very hard to find. This recipe works with those or with the conventional sweet potatoes.

166

450 g (1 lb) yams
½ cup raisins
2 tablespoons ginger, finely chopped

1½ cups spring water
2 teaspoons low-salt vegetable
  bouillon powder

If the sweet potato has a good smooth skin, simply wash and then slice crosswise. Otherwise peel and slice. Put with the other ingredients in a saucepan, cover with the water, bring to the boil and simmer for 45 minutes, adding more water if necessary and allowing the water to boil down very low towards the end. Purée the yam/raisin mixture in a food processor and serve immediately.

Orange Sauce
This orange sauce goes well with many vegetables, including green beans, cauliflower and marrow.

1 tablespoon cornflour
2 tablespoons cold water
juice of 3 medium-sized oranges
2 tablespoons of Meaux mustard
grated rind of 1 orange
3 sprigs of mint (optional)
¼ teaspoon coarsely ground black pepper

Dissolve the cornflour in the water, then add the orange juice and mustard, and heat in a saucepan until the sauce thickens. Add more orange juice if desired and toss in the rind and seasoning. Steam or blanch your choice of vegetables until cooked and then toss in the orange sauce.

SAUCES AND SPREADS
These recipes add extra flavour and texture to grain dishes, to vegetables and to salads, but some are so delicious you could eat them on their own or dip crunchy toast into them. Experiment with sauces and spreads to see what wonderful concoctions you can come up with.

Soya Cottage Cheese
Light, low in fat and simply yummy.

2 cups tofu curd
¾ cup tahini mayonnaise or
  plain mayonnaise
1 teaspoon low-salt vegetable
  bouillon powder

1 teaspoon caraway seeds
1 teaspoon mild curry powder
1 clove of garlic, chopped finely
handful of fresh herbs as
  available
2 tablespoons chopped chives

Mash the tofu well with a fork, add the other ingredients and blend. Chill before serving. This dressing will keep up to a week if refrigerated.

Raw Hummus

This works well as a dressing but, if made with less water, is also delicious spread on bread or rice cakes.

2 cups sprouted chick peas	3 tablespoons tahini
juice of 3 lemons	enough water to thin
1 teaspoon low-salt vegetable	3 teaspoons spring onions or
bouillon powder	chives, chopped
1 clove of garlic, finely chopped	

Put the ingredients (except the chives or spring onions) into a food processor or blender and blend thoroughly. Then mix in the chopped chives or spring onions and chill. This dressing will keep for 2 to 3 days in the fridge.

Aubergine Pâté

I learned this recipe from a Middle-Eastern friend who served it to me once. I had absolutely no idea what I was eating but found it completely irresistible. I have never forgotten the experience. You can vary the taste of aubergine pâté considerably by adding different spices or different extra ingredients but the principles of making it are simple. You must make sure you puncture the skins of the aubergines before baking as they will explode – this happened to me once and it blew the oven door open.

2 medium aubergines	½ cup tahini
4 cloves garlic, finely chopped	1 teaspoon low-salt vegetable
4 tablespoons fresh parsley, finely	bouillon powder or other
chopped	seasoning
1 small onion, finely chopped	½ teaspoon ground cumin
juice of 1–2 lemons	pinch of cayenne

Remove the stems from the aubergines and prick them with a fork as you would a potato. Put them into the oven and bake slowly for about 30 minutes until they become soft inside. Remove them and, being careful not to burn your fingers, scoop out the inner meat, tossing the skins away. Put into a food processor to purée. Combine all the other ingredients in the food processor with the purée, remove and chill in the fridge.

Tofu Mayonnaise

2 cups tofu	bouillon powder
2 cloves of garlic	2 teaspoons curry powder
juice of 3 lemons	2 teaspoons onion powder
1 tablespoon low-salt vegetable	pinch of salt

Put all the ingredients in a food processor and blend until smooth. If it is too thick, add a little water.

Miso Sauce

This sauce is great for cooked vegetables or tofu (which has so little flavour itself it needs quite a lot in my opinion to make it edible). This sauce uses miso which is made from fermented soya beans and rice or barley. I like the barley miso best.

$1\frac{1}{2}$ cups water

2 tablespoons arrowroot	juice of 1 lemon
$\frac{1}{2}$ cup yellow barley miso	6 tablespoons apple juice concentrate

Mix half the water together with the fruit concentrate and the miso in a food processor until thoroughly blended. Mix the arrowroot into a small amount of the remaining water and blend, adding more and more water until all the water is used up. Heat on a medium heat, stirring briskly, until the starch gels. Remove from the heat and stir in the miso mixture. Squeeze in the lemon juice at the last minute. Mix thoroughly. Serve warm or cold over hot vegetables, rice or other grains.

Cashew Sauce

This is my favourite base for all sorts of gravies. Add curry powder to it or chilli powder, or replace some of the water with tomatoes to make it an Italian sauce, adding a bit of oregano and some fresh basil and more garlic. It works for so many different dishes.

2 cups water	dash of Worcester sauce
2 cloves garlic, crushed	2 tablespoons arrowroot
2 teaspoons low-salt vegetable bouillon powder	$\frac{1}{2}$ cup raw cashews

Put all the ingredients in a food processor and blend well. Then heat gently on a stove over a medium heat until it thickens. Add more water if necessary.

Mock Cheese

This is another favourite for hamburgers or to use as a dip for fresh vegetables or to spoon on to breads or over cooked vegetables.

1 cup raw cashews	bouillon powder
1 cup hot water	1 tablespoon green onions,
3 tablespoons fresh parsley, chopped	chopped
1 large tomato	juice of 1 lemon
½ teaspoon paprika	50 g (2 oz) jar pimentos
1 teaspoon low-salt vegetable	(if you can get them)

Place all the ingredients except the chopped parsley and chopped onions in a food processor and blend until smooth. Pour the mixture into a saucepan and heat gently over a medium heat (even better on top of a bain-marie), stirring constantly until it goes thick.

You can do many variations on this theme. A little curry powder changes it into a wonderful curry sauce. A little chilli powder makes a spicy addition to any dish.

Tofu Dip

This is what I call a dip-dressing, a thick dressing which can be used as a dip or thinned a little with spring water to dress a salad.

1 cup tofu	1 teaspoon low-salt vegetable
juice of 1 lemon	bouillon powder
1 teaspoon whole-grain Meaux	a few leaves of fresh basil
mustard	and mint

Combine all the ingredients well in the food processor.

Mock Guacamole

This is a recipe I had very recently at a friend's house. I was most surprised to find out that it had been made from fresh garden peas. If you are a Guacamole lover, as I am, but don't want to eat all the fat that comes with avocados, it is a great substitute.

3 cups garden peas (you can use	½ teaspoon chilli powder
the frozen variety if you must)	1 red onion, chopped finely
3 cloves garlic, crushed	juice of 2 lemons
1 tablespoon low-salt vegetable	dash of Worcester sauce
bouillon powder	

Steam the peas lightly, being careful not to cook them too much so that they keep their brilliant colour. Purée everything but the chopped onion in a food processor then add the chopped onion and mix well by hand. Chill and serve.

SPRINKLES

Whatever your salad, whether a full mixed salad or a simple lettuce salad, it can almost certainly be improved by salad sprinkles. These can be put on to the salad or placed on the table in small dishes for people to help themselves.

Seasoned Croûtons

These are just wonderful tossed into a salad, and of course delicious dropped into a soup at the last moment.

4 slices whole-grain bread
1 tablespoon low-salt vegetable bouillon powder

1 tablespoon garlic powder
1 tablespoon onion powder

Mix the bouillon powder, garlic and onion powder into a bowl and mix well. Cut the bread into cubes and sprinkle lightly with water. Toss in the seasoning and place on a baking sheet. Either toast under a hot grill until golden and crisp or bake in a hot oven until dry. Serve hot or cold.

Toasted Sesame Topping

This is an excellent topping for vegetables and salads or to add to mock cheeses and sauces.

1½ cups sesame seeds
3 tablespoons low-salt vegetable bouillon powder

1 clove garlic, crushed
1 tablespoon onion flakes (optional)

Lightly toast the sesame seeds in a large dry pan or in the oven for 15 minutes at 150°C (300°F) Gas 2. Be sure to stir occasionally. Grind them in a food processor until fine. Add the other ingredients and continue to blend well. Sprinkle liberally over warm vegetables or fresh salads.

The Three Seeds (Living Lean)
Any or all of them – sunflower, pumpkin and sesame – as they come, ground or toasted.

Other Seeds (Living Lean)
Fennel, celery, poppy, caraway, dill, cumin (plain or toasted).

Mustard and Cress

Minced Nuts (Living Lean)

Fresh Herbs
Parsley, basil, marjoram, mint, fennel, lovage, thyme, tarragon, savory, lemon balm.

Seaweed
Nori – a type of seaweed which is dried and pressed into thin sheets. Delicious toasted and crumbled on to salad.

Flower Petals
Such as marigolds, nasturtiums, roses.

Soya Nuts (Living Lean)
These are wonderful! You simply bake soya sprouts (sprinkled with garlic powder or vegetable bouillon powder) in a moderate oven for about 15 minutes, or until brown and crunchy.

Wheat and Barley Roasts
These have a lovely sweet flavour. Bake wheat and/or barley sprouts on a baking sheet as for soya nuts.

Chick peas (Living Lean)
Cooked and cooled then tossed into a slaw or leafy salad.

Artichoke Hearts in Brine
One exception to the 'no tinned food' general rule – they are just delicious.

Finely Grated Beetroot
Adds colour to bland-looking salads.

Tofu Slices

Slices or Strips of Cold Baked Potato

Coloured Spices
Paprika, cayenne and cumin are nice dusted over pale vegetables and dressings to brighten them up.

SALADS

If you take a look at some of my salad recipes you will see that you could practically live on salads. I try to eat at least 50 per cent of my fruits and vegetables raw. Many of the Go Primitive salads are substantial whole meals, and one way of making an excellent whole-meal salad is with leftover grains or beans from the day before, mixed together with every variety of raw vegetables. Others would make delicious starters or side-dishes. They bring to the table a burst of fresh and vibrant colour and wonderful crunchy flavour. I like adding edible flowers to my salads such as marigolds and nasturtium in the summer.

Sprout Salad

This simple living salad can be completely transformed in quality depending upon the kind of dressing you serve it with. Experiment with a good tofu mayonnaise or a light Italian herbal dressing.

1 cup lentil sprouts	finely
1 cup fenugreek sprouts	3 carrots, sliced in paper-thin
1 cup alfalfa sprouts	rounds
1 cup Chinese leaves, shredded	4 tomatoes, diced

Mix the ingredients together and toss with your favourite dressing. Serve immediately.

Bulgur Salad with Endive

A delicious and substantial dish which, thanks to the endive and the bulgur wheat, is high in vitamin E. The contrast between the rich graininess of the Bulgur wheat and the delicate flavour of the endive is delightful.

450 g (1 lb) Bulgur wheat, cooked	1 tablespoon low-salt vegetable bouillon powder
2 endive	1 teaspoon balsamic vinegar
10 spring onions	3 cloves garlic, crushed
a punnet of salad cress	1 tablespoon Dijon mustard
	1 teaspoon dried tarragon leaf
For the dressing:	pinch of salt and freshly ground
3 tablespoons fresh lemon juice	black pepper to taste

Soak the Bulgur wheat overnight or for at least 3 hours in enough water to cover. Then drain excess water. Put the ingredients for the dressing into a screw-top jar and shake well until mixed. Add endive, onions and salad cress to the Bulgur wheat in a bowl and mix. Pour the dressing over the salad and toss.

Italian Salad

The Italians make some of the most delicious salads of all because they grow such splendid vegetables. When I visit Italy I buy several packets of seeds to grow different types of lettuces and basil in the garden.

1 Italian red lettuce (radicchio)	4 radishes, chopped
1 small Cos lettuce, finely shredded	1 red onion, cut into thin rings
1 red pepper, ringed	a few button mushrooms, thinly
1 yellow pepper, ringed	sliced
1–2 large Italian tomatoes, sliced	1 teaspoon fennel seeds

Make a nest of the 2 shredded lettuces in a shallow dish and arrange the other vegetables in the centre, sprinkling the onion and mushroom slices in last. Toss with a spicy Italian dressing with lots of fresh basil, and sprinkle with toasted fennel seeds and freshly ground black pepper if desired.

Jungle Slaw *(Living Lean)*
A wonderfully nutty salad full of goodness. For Quickstart simply omit the peanuts and make an oil-free dressing.

2 cups white cabbage, shredded	*½ red or yellow pepper, finely*
a handful of tender green beans,	*chopped*
raw or steamed, cut into slivers	*1 cup unsalted peanuts*
2 carrots, grated	*peanut oil*
½ onion, grated	

Combine all the ingredients except the peanuts. Make a dressing with the tiniest amount of peanut oil (if possible) and orange juice. Add the peanuts at the last minute so that they don't become soggy.

High-fibre Salad
This salad is made with a base of rice, millet or buckwheat which has been cooked and then cooled. The grains make a filling salad while supplying plenty of good-quality fibre.

2 sticks celery	*3 cups brown rice, millet*
1 carrot	*or buckwheat, cooked*
2 tomatoes	*2 spring onions*
½ red pepper	

Finely dice the celery, carrot, tomatoes and red pepper, and stir into the grain. Top with chopped spring onions. This salad works well with a vinaigrette dressing.

Winter Chunk Salad
Slaws are ideal winter salads because in the cold months when lettuce is hard to come by cabbage is a staple. Another perfect ingredient for the winter season is sprouted seeds and beans. For this salad you simply combine whatever winter vegetables and sprouts you have available and toss them together with a creamy tofu dressing.

Select three of the following	*Add a handful of mixed*
and grate: carrots, turnip,	*sprouts – mung, lentil, wheat,*
Jerusalem artichokes, kohlrabi,	*alfalfa, fenugreek or chick*
white radish, beetroot	*peas*

Combine with a handful or raisins and toss with a tofu dressing spiced with nutmeg.

Crisp Carrot Salad *(Living Lean)*
This salad has a rich, oily dressing strictly reserved for those Living Lean.

6–8 fresh carrots
3 spring onions
mustard and cress
juice of 1 lemon
juice of 1 orange
1 teaspoon whole-grain mustard

2 teaspoons honey
½ teaspoon vegetable bouillon powder
2 tablespoons olive oil
1 tablespoon fresh parsley, chopped
black pepper to taste

Scrub the carrots well and top and tail. Slice very finely cross-wise, if possible with the slicer attachment of a food processor. Finely chop the spring onions and add to the carrots along with the mustard and cress. Combine the remaining ingredients and pour over the salad. Toss well.

Apple Ginger Salad
Another very simple salad that goes with almost any dish. The ginger is a natural digest-aid.

6 green apples
¼ cup fresh orange juice
1 teaspoon fresh ginger, grated

2 teaspoons clear honey (optional)
3 tablespoons sesame seeds, toasted

Quarter the apples, remove the cores and then finely slice by hand or in a processor. Combine the orange juice, ginger and honey, and pour over the apples immediately to prevent them going brown. Add the toasted sesame seeds and toss well.

DRESSINGS
Most of the dressings I use are light and low in fat, based as they are on lemon juice, lime juice, tomato juice, orange juice and delicious herbs.

Sunny Tomato Special
A surprising combination of the tangy flavour of tomatoes sprinkled with herbs.

6 tomatoes
1 cup lima beans, cooked
2 teaspoons low-salt vegetable bouillon powder
1 clove garlic, finely chopped

juice of 2 lemons
1 tablespoon fresh parsley or basil, finely chopped (or smaller quantities of dried herbs)
dash of Worcester sauce

Put the ingredients together in a blender or food processor and blend thoroughly. The dressing will thicken as it stands. Thin with spring water if you want a thinner consistency. Chill thoroughly before use. This dressing will keep for 2 days in the fridge.

Sprout Salad Dressing

½ cup tofu or 3 medium-ripe tomatoes
½ cup fresh garden herbs
1 tablespoon sesame seeds
2 tablespoons lemon juice
1 teaspoon onion powder
1 teaspoon celery salt

Place all ingredients in a blender and mix well. Can be used as a dip or a dressing.

Tofu Vinaigrette

This is particularly nice served with artichokes.

¾ cup tofu
3 tablespoons wine vinegar
juice of 2 lemons
1 tablespoon Dijon mustard
1 clove garlic, crushed
salt and freshly ground pepper to taste

Place all ingredients in a blender and process.

Tomato Vinaigrette

This vinaigrette is particularly good on a green salad.

⅔ cup tomato juice
1 tablespoon balsamic vinegar
2 cloves garlic, crushed
1 teaspoon onion salt
10 leaves fresh basil or tarragon
pinch of salt
black pepper to taste

Blend all ingredients in a food processor, then season to taste.

Ginger Dressing

Another dip-dressing, this one has a fine hot flavour perfect for a green salad.

1 cup tofu
juice of 1 lemon
1 teaspoon lemon rind, grated
1 teaspoon honey
1 teaspoon ginger root, freshly grated
1 clove garlic, crushed
1 tablespoon red wine

Blend all the ingredients well in the food processor. Alter the quantity of red wine to adjust the thickness.

French Dressings

These dressings are especially good for leafy salads such as lettuce and spinach. With the right seasonings, such as a tasty mustard and various herbs, they can be very flavourful and not at all the 'plain oil and vineg

Basic French Dressing

¾ cup tomato juice
¼ cup lemon juice or cider vinegar
1 teaspoon whole-grain mustard
or mustard powder

a little low-salt vegetable bouillon
powder
1 clove of garlic, crushed or dried
tarragon leaf
black pepper to taste

Combine all the ingredients in a blender or simply place in a screw-top jar and shake well to mix. Some people like to thin the dressing and make it a little lighter by adding a couple of tablespoons of water.

Rich French Dressing
Add to the basic dressing:
1 tablespoon soy sauce
1 spring onion, finely chopped

a dash of cayenne

Balsamic Dressing
Add to the basic dressing:
1 tablespoon of balsamic vinegar

Herb Dressing
My favourite combination of herbs for dressings is:
3 tablespoons each of fresh
marjoram, basil, thyme, and

dill or lovage, finely chopped
(Use 2 teaspoons of each if dried)

Citrus Dressing
Use in the basic dressing:
¾ cup of seasoned tofu
juice of ½ lemon
juice of 1 orange
1 tablespoon vinegar

Add to it:
1 teaspoon orange peel, grated
½ teaspoon lemon peel, grated
pinch of nutmeg
1 teaspoon chervil

Blend all ingredients until smooth.

FRUIT TOPPINGS

Fruit toppings are great fun. They are made from fresh fruits or concentrated fruit juices. They are very easy to make and can be used in so many ways, from pouring over fruit itself to adding to morning cereals and puddings.

You can make delicious toppings and fruit sauces to go on puddings, breakfast cereals or over baked desserts by using fresh, frozen or unsweetened tinned fruits, heated together with a form of starch such as agar-agar, corn-flower or arrowroot.

Use this table to give you an idea of how much you need of each to thicken 4 cups fruit purée or fruit juice. Arrowroot works best for clear sauces. I find wheat flour, although it can be used, does not work so well with fruit but you can always use it at a pinch.

	Cornflour	Wheat flour	Arrowroot	Agar-agar
Fruit sauce or topping	2–3 tbsp	4–6 tbsp	2 tbsp	2 tbsp
Fruit pudding	⅓ cup	½ cup	4 tbsp	4 tbsp
Stewed fruit	1 tbsp	2–4 tbsp	6 tbsp	2–4 tbsp

Lucky Lemon Sauce

This sauce is delicious over fresh fruits, cakes or hot cereals. You can control the tartness by adding more or less lemon juice.

*4 medium juicy oranges, peeled
with the seeds removed or
¾ cup water with ¼ cup fruit
concentrate
2 tablespoons arrowroot*

*pinch of salt
3 tablespoons pear concentrate
juice of 2 fresh lemons
grated rind of ½ lemon
½ teaspoon ground coriander*

Place all the ingredients except the lemon juice and grated lemon rind in a food processor and blend thoroughly. Heat in a saucepan and simmer, stirring constantly, until thickened and clear. Remove from the heat and add lemon juice and lemon rind. Mix thoroughly.

Date Butter

1 cup pitted dates   *Spring water to cover*

Soak the dates in the water overnight and purée. Chill and serve. This is particularly good as a topping for desserts, and it is my favourite for spreading on bread.

Apple Butter

This is a delicious raw jam which can be used as a topping for desserts and cereals or spread on bread or toast for breakfast.

*6 apples, chopped
a handful of raisins
3 tablespoons spring water*

*1 teaspoon cinnamon
2 cloves*

Put all ingredients into a saucepan and simmer until most of the liquid has boiled away and you are left with a thick, rich apple mixture. Purée in a food processor and keep in air-tight jars.

DESSERTS

One of the great pleasures of *Lean Revolution* is being able to eat desserts again and know that all the pleasure you get from eating them will be echoed in the benefits that they can bring your body. One of my favourite desserts has always been bread pudding. I don't think I have ever enjoyed it as much as I do now, topped with some date butter or a little fruit topping. I don't eat puddings every day but, when I do, I really enjoy them.

Aaron's Delight

This is a favourite of my 12-year-old, Aaron, who has been virtually raised on fruit and sprouts. It is a very filling dish which can be eaten as a supper dish or pudding.

2 large ripe bananas　　　　　*2 tablespoons desiccated or fresh*
8 fresh dates　　　　　　　　　*grated coconut (optional)*

Put the fruit into a blender and purée until smooth. Pour into individual glass dishes. Sprinkle with fresh grated or desiccated coconut and serve.

Prune Whip

This is an excellent dish to make for breakfast or a fruit meal in the middle of winter when you have very little fresh fruit in the house. It can be made with spring water or apple juice. You may even use apple-juice concentrate mixed with a little spring water if you like.

1 cup dried prunes　　　　　　　*dash of cinnamon*
1 cup spring water or apple juice　*few slices of apple or pear*
　　　　　　　　　　　　　　　　(optional)

Soak the dried prunes overnight in apple juice or water to cover. Remove stones and blend or liquefy in a food processor with enough of the juice to make a thick sauce, adding a pinch of cinnamon. Slice a few pieces of apple or pear to use as a garnish and serve.

Pineapple Blackberry Frappé

This makes a wonderfully refreshing dessert as it stands, or can be chilled to serve as a cool sorbet on hot summer days.

2 cups fresh pineapple chunks　　*juice of ½ lime (optional)*
½ cup blackberries

Place all the ingredients in a blender and liquidize. Serve immediately.

Raspberry Ice Cream

This is the basis of all fruit ice cream. I often wash and freeze over-ripe fruit to have it ready on the spur of the moment so I can turn it into a cool, delicious dessert.

4 tablespoons agar flakes	*¼ cup apple-juice concentrate*
2½ cups soya milk	*450 g (1 lb) frozen raspberries*

Place the agar flakes and soya milk in the top of a bain-marie and boil gently, stirring constantly until the agar is dissolved. Take off the heat and pour in the apple-juice concentrate while still stirring. Add the raspberries, stir and chill. Stir the mixture from time to time until it has thickened, then freeze until firm.

Peach Ice Cream *(Living Lean only)*

Follow the same method as above but instead use:

4 cups peaches, halved	*1 cup raw cashews*
1 teaspoon vanilla essence	*1½ cups concentrated*
juice of 2 lemons	*apple juice*

Sorbet

The easiest way to make sorbets is with a sorbetière – a special machine which stirs the sorbet or ice cream as it freezes it. I have survived for many years without one by improvising.

Orange Sorbet

Remove the skin and seeds from 8 oranges and pulp them in a processor. Add a tiny amount of honey to sweeten and some nutmeg, ginger or fresh mint. I sometimes like to add a grated peach or two to give the sorbet texture. Pour the mixture into ice-cube trays or a plastic lunch-box type container and freeze. Remove from the freezer and leave to thaw slightly for about ten minutes. Blend the mixture again immediately before serving and spoon into glass dishes or into empty halved orange shells.

Strawberry or Blackberry Sorbet

Combine 3 cups of berries with 2 bananas and a little fruit juice concentrate. Follow the method as above. The bananas give a creamy texture to this sorbet.

Carob and Banana Ice Cream

This recipe is one of my family favourites. The combination of carob and honey we find unbeatable.

4 cups (about a litre or	*lecithin (optional)*
1¾ pints) soya milk	*1 cup unheated carob powder*
4 ripe bananas	*½ cup pear concentrate*
3 tablespoons granular	*1 teaspoon vanilla essence*

Freeze the milk in a low flat plastic container. When frozen, remove from the freezer and let it sit for about half an hour until it is just soft enough to slice into pieces. Put the bananas into the food processor, add about a cup of the frozen milk, the lecithin, carob powder, pear concentrate and vanilla, and blend until it is just mixed. Add the remainder of the soya milk. (Don't over-blend or you will make the ice cream too liquid.) Should it become too liquid simply return to the freezer for a few minutes then stir before serving. Serve immediately.

Stuffed Pineapple

1 large pineapple
1 orange, sliced
1 mango or papaya, chopped
1 cup raspberries or strawberries, halved
2 fresh figs, or dried ones soaked
dried coconut to garnish (optional)

Slice the pineapple in half lengthwise and remove the flesh from each half, leaving a 1 cm (½ in) shell. Dice the flesh and mix it with the sliced orange, mango/papaya and raspberries/halved straw-berries. Finely chop the figs and add. Mix all the ingredients together and spoon into the pineapple shells. Sprinkle with dried coconut and serve.

Apple Bread Pudding

Bread pudding is such a wonderful way of using practically any kind of stale bread. This works best with whole-wheat bread.

4 medium apples *12 slices bread, cubed*
2 cups soya milk or skimmed milk *1 teaspoon Amaretto*
1½ cups of raisins *¼ teaspoon freshly grated nutmeg*
2 teaspoons vanilla essence *juice of half a lemon*
½ cup concentrated apricot juice *pinch of salt*

Mix the soya milk together with the apricot concentrate, vanilla essence and salt. Tear the bread into small cubes and mash it into the milk mixture. Allow to soak for 15 minutes. In another bowl combine the apple, raisins, lemon juice and Amaretto. Add to the bread mixture and toss gently. Pour into a non-stick baking pan, sprinkle with nutmeg, and cook in a pre-heated oven at 180°C (350°F) Gas 4 for 45 minutes or until set and browned on top. Serve warm.

Rice Pudding

Another old-time favourite which my family likes to eat not only as a sweet but also for breakfast.

2 cups cooked brown rice	3 teaspoons lemon juice
¾ cup soya milk or skimmed milk	grated rind of 1 lemon
1 teaspoon cinnamon	pinch of salt
1 teaspoon vanilla essence	½ cup raisins
¼ cup concentrated pear or	shredded coconut (optional)
apple juice	

Mix all the ingredients (except the coconut) together and bake for 45 minutes at 180°C (350°F) Gas 4. Serve with soya or skimmed milk. You can top with coconut if you wish.

Baked Apples

4 large apples	(optional)
½ cup date butter or raisins that	2 tablespoons vanilla essence
have been soaked in water for	2 tablespoons rum (optional)
2 hours or more	2 tablespoons fresh lime or
¼ cup chopped almonds or pecans	lemon juice

Wash and core the apples. Mix other ingredients together in a small bowl and stuff the core of each apple. Place in a non-stick oven dish and pour remaining mixture over the apples, adding a tablespoon or two of water if necessary. Bake for 45 minutes at 180°C (350F) Gas 4.

Pie Crust

This is a wholesome base for any sort of fruit pie you can come up with – experiment with pouring fruit sauces and toppings over fresh fruit and baking.

¾ cup finely ground flour –	¼ cup spring water
barley or rice flours are best	⅓ cup almond or cashew butter
⅓ teaspoon salt	

Put all the dry ingredients into a bowl and add the water a little at a time, mixing to a firm dough. Press on to a pie plate or in to a pie dish, prick with a fork and bake at 180°C (350°F) Gas 4 until lightly browned. Fill with your favourite filling.

Granola Crust

This is a lovely crumbly crust using breakfast granola as a base.

3 cups granola, ground finely	3–6 tablespoons water
2 teaspoons cinnamon	2 tablespoons fruit concentrate

Put the ground granola and cinnamon in a bowl. Add the fruit concentrate and mix well, adding water a little at a time until you have a dough. Press on to a pie plate and bake at 180°C (350°F) Gas 4 for 30 minutes until browned.

Lemon Pie

This is my favourite. It is tart and refreshing, particularly good on a dull winter's day.

Baked Pie Crust (see recipe)
3 cups water
7 tablespoons arrowroot
⅔ cup fruit juice concentrate
3 tablespoons lemon rind
juice of 2 lemons

⅔ cup cashew nuts
⅓ cup coconut (optional)
¼ teaspoon salt
1 dozen mint leaves
*3 teaspoons Cointreau or
    Amaretto*

Put all the ingredients except the lemon juice and liqueur into a food processor and blend until smooth. Put into a shallow pan and heat gently, stirring constantly until thick. Add the lemon juice and the liqueur and pour into a baked pie shell. Allow to set in the fridge and top with grated coconut.

Banana Cream Pie

This is a traditional American dish and one that I particularly enjoy making.

Baked Pie Crust (see recipe)
4 cups soya milk
4 ripe bananas
½ cup arrowroot

2 tablespoons fruit concentrate
1 teaspoon vanilla essence
¼ teaspoon salt

Put into a saucepan the milk, fruit concentrate, vanilla essence, salt and arrowroot and heat gently, stirring constantly until thick. Take off the heat. Purée two of the bananas and stir into the milk mixture. Slice the other bananas and layer into the pie crust. Finally, pour the milk mixture over the bananas and chill until set.

Resources

REAL FOODS

The best supermarkets carry a good selection of beans, pulses and grains, so do cash and carry wholesalers, many of whom also sell to the public in bulk. Here are a few of my favourite outlets. To find your local suppliers, contact your nearest health-food shop for details.

Alara Wholesale,
Units 4–5,
Camley Street,
London NW1 1XX.
Tel: 071-387 9303
(Do not deliver)

Community Foods Ltd,
Micross,
Brent Terrace,
London NW2 1LT.
Tel: 081-450 9411

Green City Wholefoods,
23 Flemming Street,
Glasgow G31 1PQ.
Tel: 041-554 7633

House of Goodness,
South March,
Daventry,
Northants NN11 4PH.
Tel: 0327 706611
(Minimum order around
£250)

Infinity Wholesale,
67 Norway Street,
Portslade,
Brighton,
East Sussex BN4 1AE.
Tel: 0273-424060

Marigold Foods,
Unit 10
St Pancras Commercial
  Centre,
63 Pratt Street,
London NW1 0BY.
Tel: 071-267 7368

Neals Yard Wholefood
  Warehouse,
21 Shorts Gardens,
London WC2H 9AS.
Tel: 071-836 5151
or
Unit 5,
Chelsea Farmers Market,
Sydney Street,
London SW3 6PU.
Tel: 071-352 6006
(Not a wholesaler but a good
retail emporium where you
can buy in bulk)

Suma Wholefoods,
Dean Clough,
Halifax HX3 5AN.
Tel: 0422 345513

Survival Foods,
Unit 2,
Cobnash Road,
Kingsland,
Herefordshire HR6 9RW.
Tel: 0568 708 344

Coffee substitute: My favourite coffee substitute is dandelion coffee, the sort that you grind like coffee beans and use in the same way in a filter coffee maker or cafetière. For your nearest stockist, contact Cotswold Health Works Ltd, 5–6 Tabernacle Road, Watton Under Edge, Gloucestershire GL12 7EF. Tel: 0453 843 694.

Digestive enzymes: If you find you have trouble digesting carbohydrates, a carbohydrate enzyme food supplement such as Carbozyme can be very useful. For details of where to obtain Carbozyme, contact BioCare Ltd, 54 Northfield Road, Kings Norton, Birmingham B30 1JH. Tel: 021 433 3727

Evening primrose oil: Nature's Own do a very good pure Evening Primrose Oil (not a blend) which is cold pressed, is free from herbicides or pesticides, and is non-solvent extracted. So do Solgar and Health Innovations (see below). It is sold in capsules by Nature's Own and also in a liquid dropper for vegetarians from Nature's Own, 203–205 West Malvern Road, West Malvern, Worcs WR14 4BB. Tel: 0684 892 555; Fax 0684 892 643.

Flaxseeds and linseeds: Linusit Gold are the best linseeds. Vacuumed-packed whole linseeds (or flaxseeds) are available in most health-food stores.

Glycosport and Glycoslim energy supplements: Available in Holland & Barrett, good sports clubs or by post from Health Innovations, Unit 10, Riverside Business Centre, Brighton Road, Shoreham, West Sussex BN43 6RE. Tel: 0273 440 177; Fax 0273 465 325.

Green barley: Available in powder form to make delicious drinks with freshly squeezed fruit juice from: Xynergy, Ash House, Stedham, Midhurst, West Sussex GU29 0PT. Tel: 0730 813 642.

Herb teas: Some of my favourite blends include Cinnamon Rose, Orange Zinger and Emperor's Choice by Celestial Seasonings; Warm and Spicy by Symingtons; and Creamy Carob French Vanilla. Yogi tea, by Golden Temple Products, is a strong spicy blend perfect as a coffee replacement.

Marigold Swiss vegetable bouillon: This instant broth powder based on vegetables and sea salt is available from health-food stores or direct from Marigold Foods, Unit 10, St Pancras

Commercial Centre, 63 Pratt Street, London NW1 0BY. Tel: 071-267 7368. It comes in regular and low-salt forms. The low-salt form is excellent for making spirulina broth.

Nutritional supplements: I like the nutritional supplements from Solgar. They do an excellent EPA/DHA supplement for the Omega 3 fatty acids, called Omega-3 700 Softgels, and a good chlorella supplement. Solgar also do excellent multiple vitamins and minerals; my favourite is their VM2000. Solgar Vitamins Ltd, PO Box 398, Chesham, Bucks HP5 3EY. Tel: 0494 791 691. For lower potency supplements with high bio-availability, Nature's Own do unique vitamins which, through a patented process, have been bonded to food proteins to render them highly bio-available; their minerals are put through a biotec process that organically ties them to a food matrix. So special is this process of *renaturing* and so thorough are the studies – published and unpublished on their products – that many of their supplements are treated as prescribable by doctors. They do an excellent Vitamin B-Complex, good niacin, Beta Carotene, Calcium and Magnesium, as well as other single vitamins and minerals. For shops nearest to you, tel: 0684 892 555.

Organic meat: For excellent venison and wild boar in cuts of meat, burgers and sausages, low in fat and full of taste, Fletchers Fine Foods, Reediehill, Auchtermuchty, Fife KY14 7HS. Tel: 0337 28369.

Water: Friends of the Earth have an excellent briefing sheet, 'Drinking water: is it up to standard?' Contact Friends of the Earth, 26–28 Underwood Street, London N1 7JQ.

Sea plants for cooking and salads: Can be bought from Japanese grocers or macrobiotic health shops.

Spirulina: Available in powder form to make into delicious drinks with freshly squeezed fruit juice from: Xynergy, Ash House, Stedham, Midhurst, West Sussex GU29 0PT. Tel: 0730 813 642.

USEFUL ADDRESSES

Weimar Institute, PO Box 486, 20601 West Paoli Lane, Weimar, CA 95736, USA. Tel: 916 637 4111.
and
Colgan Institute of Nutritional Science, 565 Pearl Street, Suite 301, La Jolla, CA 92037, USA. Tel: 619 632 7722.

Country Life Restaurants
If you want to try Lean Revolution foods, have lunch at one of the Country Life restaurants which are inexpensive and excellent.

Country Life London, 123 Regent Street Building, 1 Heddon Street, London W1. Tel: 071-434 2922

Country Life Basel,
Andreasplatz 12,
4051 Basel,
Switzerland.
Tel: 41 61 25 09 39

Country Life Marseille,
14 Rue Venture,
13001 Marseille,
France.
Tel: 33 91 54 16 44

Country Life Paris,
6 Rue Daunou,
75002 Paris,
France.
Tel: 33 14 29 74 851

Country Life Prague,
Melantrichova 15,
Prague 1,
Czech Republic.
Tel: 422 22 53 78

Country Life Osaka,
Saiwai Building, B1,
2–13 Kitahama-Higashi,
Chuoku, Osaka 540,
Japan.
Tel: 816 943 9597

A-Chee-Nee Restaurant,
Gun Gang Sik Dang,
#269-21 Jui Kyung-Dong,
Dong Dae Moon-Ku,
Seoul,
Korea 131-00.
Tel: 82 25245 0912

Living Springs Restaurant,
116 East 60th Street,
New York,
NY 10022, USA.
Tel: 212 319 7850/9263

Country Life Los Angeles,
88 S. Figueroa Street,
Los Angeles, CA 90017, USA.
Tel: 213 489 4118

FURTHER READING

The complete list of references – over three hundred – fills a little book of its own. I have given here the core books for further reading; if you would like the full list of references, chapter by chapter, please send an A4 SAE to the publisher's address.

Good Cook Books

A Good Cook... Ten Talents by Frank J. Hurd DC & Rosalie Hurd BS, Dr & Mrs Frank J Hurd, Box 86A – Route 1, Chisholm, Minnesota 55719, USA, 1968

Country Life Natural Foods. Something Better, Nutrition Seminar Cookbook, MMI Press, Aldworth Road, Box 279, Harrisville, NH 03450, USA, 1984

Country Life Vegetarian Cookbook, edited by Diana J. Flemming, Family Health Publications, 13062 Musgrove Highway, Sunfield, Michigan 48890, USA, 1990

Eat For Strength. A Vegetarian Cookbook by Agatha Thrash MD, New Lifestyle Books, Route 1, Box 441, Seale, AL 36875, USA, 1978

Recipes from the Weimar Kitchen, Weimar Institute, PO Box 486, Weimar, CA 95736-0486, USA, 1992

Good Books on Health

Diet for a Poisoned Planet by David Steinman, Ballantine Books, New York, USA 1990

Diet for a Small Planet by Frances Moore Lappé, Ballantine, New York, USA, 1971

Newstart! by Vernon Foster MD, Woodbridge Press, CA, USA, 1990

Nutrition and Health by Sir Robert McCarrison, The McCarrison Society, London, 1953

Nutrition for the Nineties by Winston J. Craig, Golden Harvest Books, Michigan, USA, 1992

Nutrition for Vegetarians by A.M. and C.L. Thrash, Thrash Publications, Seale, Alabama, USA, 1982

Optimum Sports Nutrition by Michael Colgan, Advanced Research Press, New York, USA, 1993

Reversing Heart Disease by Dr Dean Ornish, Random Century, London, 1991

Silent Spring by Rachel Carson, Penguin, London, 1962

The Lean Body Promise by Dr Vince Quas, Synesis Press, Oregon, USA, 1989

Why George Should Eat Broccoli by Paul Sitt, The Dougherty Company, Wisconsin, USA, 1990

Your Personal Vitamin Profile by Michael Colgan MD, Morrow, New York, USA, 1982

Index